The Lily and the Lotus

By

Philippa Groves

 **New Generation Publishing**

This is an honest and personal account of my own experience and does not necessarily represent the views of any of the organizations mentioned below.

Chapter 1

FIRST THERE WERE BOOKS - THEN THERE WERE LAMAS

I didn't feel as if I belonged on the South Coast. I belonged in the North East, where the cold wind blows thinly, driving salt water into face and hair. I would miss my wild coastal haunts with birds and plants that would not wish to live on the hot pebbly beaches or concrete promenades in Hastings. But for now it would have to do as Paula and I needed a home.

The events of the previous year had opened up my mind to new possibilities and I could no longer trust or follow blindly the values which had led me to this point. I needed to move away from the safety of my familiar beliefs, the dead end of conformity.

It was time to seek my own path and I remembered I was not born a Catholic; I was baptised a Catholic.

The liberating decision not to follow the Catholicism of my childhood had not been taken lightly but it made me feel lighter.

I live like a butterfly in a jam jar
A captive spirit longing to be free
I long to feel the air upon my wings
To bathe in sun again
But captive though I am
I know I can be free

Like many children I caught insects and kept them in jars as my pets and just like these poor butterflies, I had spent so much of my life within the confines of the Catholic Church, trapped by the expectations of others.

My little prisoners had a right to be free, and so did I. I now realised, just like me, these little insects had not wished to be trapped.

This was the time to free myself from the jam jar of my own limitations.

I had seen a newspaper advert placed by a Humanist organisation and decided to investigate. Tingling with excitement I wrote for information and soon received some literature, which included a simple form with twelve questions, each one having a box to tick. As far as I recall I had no problem with eleven of the questions, but I could not answer the most important one as to whether I believed in an afterlife. The Humanists clearly held that this life is the only one we have and, when we die, we go out like spent fireworks. But could it be that simple?

If I had been able to answer this to *their* satisfaction, I could have sent off for a sweet little *happy man* badge; happy because he is unburdened with worries about life after death.

Of course I wanted to be happy, but since I could not state categorically there was no afterlife, I couldn't wear the happy man badge.

My short excursion into Humanism ended almost as soon as it began, but it did serve to highlight I still had some religious conviction. I could no longer believe in the Catholic Heaven with its angels, but nor did I believe that death was the end, although I was still unsure of what an afterlife was really like.

The junior school mistress, Mrs Duffy, had given the advice we should treat others as *we* would wish to be treated ourselves. That was good advice, and I had seen that it worked in practice; but there had to be a deeper meaning to life than that.

When I was told that I would go blind, it had taken away my confidence to paint. How could I continue to paint when before long I would not be able to see anything?

However, in nineteen-seventy six, a friend gave me a large canvas for Christmas, and after many months wondering what to paint on it, I had a wonderful dream which was made up of ideas rather than images, when I woke up I wanted to paint the dream, but how could I represent a *Circle of Life* in oils. My paintings usually didn't carry titles, but this one certainly would.

In front of a golden orb of the sun, two birds danced ecstatically, a flurry of freedom and feathers, symbolising unity; while in the right corner I stood in a yellow dress encircled by horses. If I was a lover of horses that would have been wonderful, but I feared being trapped by this powerful circle and could find no way out.

To represent the orb, I had painted the blue birds circling in front of a bright yellow sun. More Marc Chagall than Modigliani. That seemed strange, as my favourite painter was Modigliani and the style was very different to anything I had painted before. However, coincidentally, Marc Chagall often painted dreams of brides flying through the sky in front of a bright sun.

Until then I had given his paintings little thought as I liked to cover the whole canvas with a thick oily layer of paint; while Chagall left much of his canvas bare. I now realised painting was the most important thing in my life. The purpose was not to attract galleries or buyers; it was done simply for its own sake. When I painted I became so absorbed in my work that time stopped. It was pure experience, and I could not imagine anything that could be more precious than that feeling.

After completing this painting, from the depths of my heart I implored the Unknown to offer me something, which could take the place of painting.

Only then could I let it go without a devastating feeling of loss.

It was not long after making this prayer that I had a dream of a gothic cathedral with twin turrets. When I awoke I knew I had to find this building. Never before had I felt the need to act upon a dream in waking life. Dreams belonged to my sleep and, although they could leave a lingering feeling of well-being or anxiety after I woke up, they did not usually influence my waking life.

But in the search for this dream cathedral, I described it to several people and asked if they knew where to look? Generally they were not keen to get involved in my search for a phantom cathedral.

However illogical it might have seemed to others, I had no doubt that it was a real building, and that sooner or later I would visit it.

Shortly after this dream I became ill and unable to sleep. I had read all the books on my shelves except one my sister Jean had left while she travelled abroad.

I had never heard of the author and the title – *Walk On* – was not very inspiring, but as it had found its way onto my bookshelf it would have to do. I picked up the faded old book and began to read. As far as I recall, each chapter began with the words 'Walk on' and offered advice on beginning a spiritual journey into Buddhism. Though I remember little about the book it grabbed my attention enough to begin my own journey into the study of the Buddhist faith.

In great excitement at the prospect of learning more, I wrote to the address on the back cover and explained I felt the author was talking down to the reader. How was I to know that he was a high court judge and the founder of the Buddhist Society? To me he just seemed to be lecturing his reader in a rather superior manner, and I did not wish to know any more about him. But what he had to say was quite amazing, and so I asked them if they could tell me more about the Buddhist religion.

They sent an impressive package of information. There were several small books, including one called the *Dhammapada*. There was also information about a short introductory postal course on Buddhism, and an invitation to the monthly Saturday afternoon tea party and talk at the Buddhist Society. I felt destined to go.

So I signed up for the correspondence course and the following Saturday went to the tea party. The talk was by Christmas Humphries QC 1901-1983, the author of *Walk On.* I hoped no one had told him I thought his book a boring exposition of a very interesting subject. I don't recall much of his talk, but I do remember wondering about the stuffed parrot on the table in the library, as well as the Cadbury's chocolate finger I ate at the tea party – the rest of the food having quickly disappeared while I talked to a small group of people.

I went home filled with excitement about this day and the possibilities which lay ahead. At last I had met people who thought the same way as I did.

On the correspondence course I read a little about reincarnation, something I had never heard of before. One thing that particularly intrigued me was the statement that all the suffering we experience during this life comes from our having taken rebirth as a human being; yet it is this very same human rebirth that is the best basis for overcoming all suffering. This was exciting news. My adventure was beginning.

First I thought that I had better study the idea of reincarnation, so for the first time in my life I deliberately set out to disobey the advice of the Catholic Church and my mother, who strongly disapproved of what she perceived as fake faiths. This act, which would possibly have no significance for most people, was for me as exciting as a childhood adventure.

As such, risking Hell and damnation, I made an appointment with a palmist and, looking over my shoulder to make sure my mother was not watching me, sneaked onto Hastings pier and to the gaily painted door displaying photographs of famous people holding out their palms to be read by 'Gypsy Rose the Genuine Romany Gypsy.'

Gypsy Rose was indeed a very sincere lady. She didn't tell me much about reincarnation but she did say that my karma was speeding up, not that this meant anything to me, and then she told me a few things about this life, including information about my childhood which she could not have known by any ordinary means. She insisted that in a few weeks time I would move to a very large building with big windows and two separate gateways up to the imposing front door, 'Where you will be very happy,' she said.

Although Gypsy Rose had not told me anything about life before birth or after death, she did convince me that there was a state of consciousness – a perspective or viewing point, beyond what most people saw in their day-to-day life.

Though reincarnation was a new idea to me, it began to make complete sense. It was like the missing part of the jigsaw of life. To suddenly appear on earth as a baby, a unique child different from everyone else did not add up to me. Why are some people born as geniuses or with rich and famous parents while others are born disabled and in poverty? If God loved us all equally, we should surely come into this world with equal opportunities? But this is not how it is. If there is any justice in the world, the only explanation is that we must have brought this potential for good or bad conditions from our own past lives, so why feel guilty about them now? This potential for good or bad conditions in life is what Buddhists call our karma. We create our karma through our good and bad deeds, but once we have created it we cannot escape it. It will follow us from life to life, shaping our destiny. When this life ends we won't just be sent to Heaven or Hell for an eternity, but we will be reincarnated into lives shaped by the karma we ourselves have created. In comparison to the expansive idea of reincarnation, I now found the Christian view of the afterlife rather limited and odd. I could no longer just be a local girl. I had become a global person. Perhaps in the past I had been a man or an animal, or perhaps even a fly!

Whatever the past had held for me all I could do now was live here in this female body and try to create good causes for a better future. The thought of infinite lives in unlimited places was quite frightening at first. I wanted to cling more tightly to my familiar surroundings and family and friends rather than be swept away by the tide of karma and thrown into an unknown future. Although I did not feel worthy of going there, the concept of Heaven seemed a more comforting idea.

It seemed to me, we come into this life as a 'person kit' and are glued together by our parents at conception. And although we come in kit form and assemble our life from the parts in our own unique kit, sometimes a few parts are the wrong size, sub-standard or are missing altogether, as we have not created the cause to have them in this life.

The collection is our body, mind and personality. Of course we have certain features acquired from our parents, and some of our values and mannerisms are also formed through their influence, but most things are brought with us from a past life rather than being acquired in this one. This can be seen very clearly in the case of a musical genius born into a poor family who has no interest in music or art and is possibly even tone deaf.

So life *is* fair. Life in fact cannot be unfair. Did I find this statement shocking or liberating? Perhaps both. It was shocking and very difficult to accept I myself had created every bit of suffering I had encountered in this life. Nevertheless the idea that most of my problems of this life had their origins in my own actions in past lives made more sense than saying it is all due to the unfathomable will of God, which made my suffering little more than the indiscriminate handing out of punishment. Now I could apply the new logic I had read about in books on Buddhism to the unfathomable and see if I could make more sense of my life. The Buddhist understanding of the state beyond death was far more comprehensive than that of the Catholicism I had grown up with, and I found it easier to accept.

To understand the Buddhist idea of what happens after death, I first needed to understand the twin beliefs of karma and rebirth. These concepts made complete sense to me; their logic seemed watertight; yet was open to scrutiny in a way that was the opposite of the ideas behind unquestioning faith.

In fact one of the first things that attracted me to Buddhism was Buddha's statement, 'Believe nothing that I have said, until you have tried it for yourself'.

Having some understanding of the past and future would give me control of the present. How exciting life was becoming now. Baptism of a defenceless child before it could talk had never felt right.

As a Catholic child I was taught to believe there is a special place called limbo reserved for babies who die before they are baptised, and where they are kept waiting for a while before they go to Heaven. Baptised adults who die having committed only venial sins go to purgatory until these sins have been purged through suffering, and then they also go to Heaven. Those who during their life have committed a Mortal Sin will spend the rest of eternity burning in Hell.

On the surface there seemed to be similarities between this and what I had read about Buddhism. Instead of limbo, there is a state called the bardo, a state between this life and the next. But it was not reserved just for babies. And instead of purgatory there are the lower rebirths in which through suffering, negative karma is gradually burned up. Buddhism also talks about Hell, but unlike the Catholic version of Hell, it is not eternal and so in some ways is more like purgatory.

My understanding of the Buddhist conception of the afterlife was very muddled at the time, and was not helped by the scarcity of good, easy-to-read books. One of the topics which confused me was the Buddhist belief in many gods. I had been brought up to believe that there is just one God who lives forever in Heaven. But Buddhism talked about a multitude of gods who have exceptionally long lives in Heaven, filled with all kinds of pleasure, but who, in the end, die in extreme anguish because they see the place where they will take rebirth, which almost certainly will be in a lower state as they have used up most of their good karma in godly pleasures.

I found the idea of a dead God shocking, as shocking as the idea of many gods or of becoming a god myself. But giving this idea a little thought and removing some of the prejudice in my mind it made perfect sense. After all, Catholicism had taught me that I could go to Heaven, and if we call the inhabitants of Heaven 'gods' then it was not so different. Suppose I went to Heaven but did not make any effort to improve myself spiritually, spending all my time simply enjoying Celestial pleasures? Surely there would be a time when I ran out of good karma and no longer deserved to be in Heaven?

Little by little the Buddhist conception of Heaven as a pleasant but temporary state began to make sense. Gradually I found myself drawn towards books which described the Buddhism of Tibet. These were magical books. The first author who captured my imagination was John Blofeld (1913-1987) an Englishman who had travelled extensively around Asia and met many Lamas during his travels. – Author of *The Tantric Mysticism of Tibet*, 1970.

For me this book was decisive and now I sought out books describing the Buddhism of Tibet.

Another such author was Lama Anagarika Govinda (1898-1985) and his book *The Way of the White Clouds* described his travels in Tibet and India. Reading this book had a profound effect and while reading it I could almost smell the grass and feel the chill in the air of the land of the snows.

After reading these books, I often asked my correspondence course tutor questions about Tibetan Buddhism. As she did not know the answers she passed these questions on to a Tibetan Lama called Lama Chime Rinpoche, one of the first Lamas to live in England, and then relayed his answers back to me. She explained that she was a Theravadin Buddhist; so did not know much about Tibetan Buddhism and suggested that I visit a Buddhist Centre in Cumbria called The Manjushri Institute, which had just opened. She told me that a friend of hers, a true seeker, had visited it and spoke very highly of it.

Hearing that there were some Tibetan Lamas living in England was exciting news as I felt the need to meet a Lama in person but had not dared dream of a trip to India to seek one out.

The first Lama I visited was Lama Chime Rinpoche who had established a centre in Saffron Walden. During my visit to Marpa House in Saffron Walden I spent the weekend with several other Westerners. All had a little more familiarity with Tibetans and Buddhism than I had. However, apart from one Tara meditation each day in a small room with several cushions on the floor, there was little to do. People just seemed to hang out there.

For periods of up to three years. Occasionally the Lama would give a weekend course. On the weekend of my visit he was not teaching but offered to give interviews to anyone who wanted to talk to him. Determined to find out more about Buddhism, I made an appointment to see him. This was to be my first encounter with a real live Tibetan Lama; I was nervous but excited at the same time. Unfortunately I did not understand much of his English. The only thing I understood was that I should read a book called *Cutting through Spiritual Materialism* by Chogyam Trungpa Rinpoche, which I did.

Meals were vegetarian and self-service in a large dining room. Although the food was simple, the company was anything but. There were one or two old timers who had been to India and were regulars at the Buddhist Society Summer School. I envied them their travels, but my observation that Buddhists would need to live in a Buddhist Centre to practice properly in the West did not go down well with these particular people.

The following morning at breakfast a young man wearing a maroon bow tie and suit under which he wore a chunky red hand knitted sweater took us all by surprise when he began to chant mantras loudly over his cornflakes in a wonderful deep voice. He certainly set the mood, but what was this about? Being English we chose not to notice his unconventional behaviour and concentrated on eating our food.

After breakfast one of the volunteer workers came through from the office and asked me to give her my name and address for the visitor's book. Afterwards I realised that I had written only my address. Where had Philippa gone? Thinking how this place with its lack of structure had affected me, I became helpless with laughter. Had I ceased to be a person in this short time? The Buddhist books I had found in local bookshops had spoken of emptiness, but the concept of emptiness was too obscure for me to grasp. Unseen and unknown, I felt that it might be similar to the concept of God that I had tried to understand before my first Holy Communion. But God and emptiness were different. God did nothing; emptiness was nothing.

I paid, packed and went home to take stock of the weekend. I could not deny it was different from anything else I had experienced, but did not feel the need to return.

A few weeks later I received the *Middle Way Journal* which was produced by the Buddhist Society. The centre pages were filled with a picture of Manjushri Institute in Cumbria, a huge gothic building graced by twin turrets. It was without a doubt the building in my dream. More exciting still, the advert was to invite new residents to live there and work in the community and study Buddhism with a Tibetan Lama.

My search was now over, but where would I ever find the money to visit this Gothic priory, the building in my dream?

Now I knew where it was, I only had to work out when and how I could go. There was a lot to consider, as my daughter Paula was still young and needed a school and I wanted to work as a potter. I was not sure what the resident Buddhists would feel about a partially sighted single mum with a seven year-old girl and only a very superficial knowledge of Buddhism gleaned from books. Although much of what I had read was incomprehensible; whenever I read books about Tibet or Tibetan Buddhism I felt an inexplicable familiarity and inspiration. I was convinced that Tibetan Buddhism was for me. But my main concern was, 'What had I to offer these dedicated Buddhists, who had come from all over the Western world after studying with Tibetan Lamas in India?'

Some even spoke fluent Tibetan and could read and write it. Compared to them I knew nothing. What would these people expect of me? I sent them a poem expressing my desire to find the meaning of life and hoped it was enough to satisfy them.

I had now completed my training course in Torquay run by the R.N.I.B (Royal National Institute for the Blind) where I had trained to be a potter.

Now I planned to set up my own pottery and make Buddha figures as well as more saleable objects.

During my stay in Torquay, I had the opportunity to visit the Golden Rosary Hermitage in Lostwithiel a few times. Understanding the benefits of living near other spiritual practitioners, I asked the residents of the hermitage to try to help me find suitable accommodation in the area. At the same time, however, I was looking for somewhere to live near Manjushri Institute. I planned to move to whichever one offered some accommodation.

Before I left Torquay I had asked my course tutor to contact someone in Cumbria to help me with my pottery when I moved as this was what they had recommended during my training. At first they explained their job was just to assess me for work and recommend a career. But at my insistence they contacted a rehabilitation officer. Who advised me to get in touch as soon as I moved.

On a freezing day in February 1979, Paula and I caught the train from Hastings for our long awaited first visit to Manjushri Institute, arriving in Ulverston late that evening – the cold, ice and snow not disturbing us at all.

During our visit, Roy, the secretary, asked me if I wished to visit Geshe Kelsang. I had not a clue what to expect but it sounded like something people did when they visited and, so as not to seem too ignorant, I said I would like to attend.

Paula and I went into the small, poorly lit room and prostrated ourselves in front of the Lama as we had been advised. He was a slightly built man with a shy, gentle smile, dressed in classic Tibetan red Buddhist robes, and sitting quietly cross-legged in the centre of his gold candlewick bedspread. He greeted us in Tibetan. With the aid of his translator we were invited to sit down in front of him on the floor. I looked around the room. Apart from the bed and a small table under the window with a single chair, the only furniture was a shelf above the bed filled with religious texts and a small chest of drawers on which there was an altar with seven brass bowls filled with water arranged in front of a few brass Buddha statues so highly polished that they glinted in the subdued light. The translator, Tenzin Norbu, sat on the floor in front of us. After introducing us he then asked what we wished to say to Geshe-la. I had no idea what to say. I was asked how much I knew about Buddhism. It was obvious I knew very little. So Geshe-la recommended I read some books and gave me advice on my diet. We received his blessing and he said he would pray for my eyesight to improve. He then gave Paula a box of chocolates. We thanked him and quietly left the room. This was my second visit to a Tibetan Lama and on both occasions I was impressed by the lack of opulence and the simplicity of lifestyle.

During my visit to Manjushri, a local estate agent telephoned the Institute to say there was a flat available a short walk away. The flat was not large but it would certainly do, and six weeks later we moved in.

Sadly, after I moved I discovered that the rehabilitation officer who had promised to help me set up my pottery had died, and there was no one to take his place.

I tried to set up the pottery myself until someone from the government came and asked me to sign a form declaring that I was doing no work, either paid or unpaid. So there were to be no Buddha statues at this time. As we were not rich Paula and I walked everywhere. On Saturdays, when we went to town and sat down in *Salmon's* warm cafe for lunch, my eyes would close with tiredness and Paula would scold me, saying 'Mum don't meditate here!'

When the summer holidays came, we hitched into the Lake District, and camped by the shores of Derwent Water where several years ago I had spent the whole winter sketching and painting; when Paula was just a toddler. Our cheap little backpacker tent always let in the rain, but the freedom it gave us was very special as now the snow had been replaced by a soft summer breeze and warm sunshine.

Paula looked good walking ahead with a sizeable rucksack on her back, while I walked behind, carrying the heavier things. Perhaps some day we would go on a real holiday but I could not imagine a better place to relax than among the sheep and lambs in the Lakeland fells.

Paula wanted to see her Dad, and so went to stay with him in Newcastle. Then, when my health did not improve, my brother David invited her to live in Hastings with his family. I was delighted she was going to share in a real family life with her two younger cousins; my bronchitis still troubled me so I had to avoid winter trips, only travelling south in the warm summer months to visit her.

At some point my mother decided I should move back to live with Paula on the South Coast. She explained that initially I was to live in her flat and Paula would continue to live with David, until they found me a flat. Was I still a child? Did I have to obey my mother now?

She said she would not stop me from being a Buddhist and told me that I could visit a Buddhist monastery in Sussex. Should I tell her that I would not stop her being a Christian but she really need not trouble herself to walk twenty minutes to attend the Catholic Church when the C of E Church is just over the road from her?

I thanked her, and realising she would not understand my reason for living in this unique international Buddhist community in Cumbria, I simply told her I was too selfish to move south. This was one of those occasions when there is not enough common ground to have a reasonable debate. I love debate but there are times when it is not appropriate as the person is not open to new ideas and would only get upset. She had her views and I mine.

The more I understood Buddhist philosophy, the more I appreciated other faiths. Though I hadn't studied other religions in any depth, I intuitively felt in the distant past they must have had a lot more in common than they seem to have now.

It was difficult to explain to my mother why the Buddhist monastery in Sussex could not take the place of Manjushri Institute for me. The monastery belonged to the Theravada school of Buddhism, whereas Manjushri Institute was part of the Mahayana school. Both schools were taught by Buddha and are still to be respected.

I had the good fortune to do a couple of short Theravadan retreats in Harnham Vihara near Newcastle, which I found wonderful and full of loving people. But there are important differences between the two schools.

There is a wonderful Tibetan story of a blind man who was up in a mountain pasture tending his family's yaks. When he wanted to return to his village in the evening all he needed to do was to take hold of the tail of one of the yaks from his village and follow it home. If halfway down he caught hold of the tail of a different yak, there would be no knowing where he would end up.

I am a partially sighted woman and have chosen my yak. I am sure that if I follow this yak, my chosen Buddhist tradition, I will finally reach my true home of Buddhahood. But if I swap traditions I will just get lost. So I held tightly to the yak's tail and remained alone in Cumbria, while Paula returned south with Mum. I missed Paula a lot but I was sure she would have a better quality of life than I could provide for her. I hoped when she was more independent she would return to Cumbria.

Chapter 2

REFUGE

During The Easter holiday, there was a Lamrim (Graduated Path to Enlightenment) retreat for beginners in the Oak Room and I was determined to take part. Most of the students were visitors who had come for a week, as the residents were more familiar with basic Buddhist ideas and also were too busy working for the Institute. But I did not have to work and took every opportunity to deepen my knowledge of Buddhism, so I was delighted that Tubten Angmo, an American nun who had spent some time in India with Tibetan Lamas, was going to teach a basic meditation course this week.

She began by introducing the idea of karma - the law of cause and effect. Normally we see all of our problems coming from outside and created by other people or conditions beyond our control, but she continued, it is only if we get upset that we have a problem. The real problem, therefore, is the unpleasant feeling in our mind, it exists inside us not outside. This way of looking at life was certainly very different to the beliefs of my childhood and was so new; I was well aware that it would take time to understand it.

Buddha had discovered how to free himself from his own inner problems and taught others how to follow in his footsteps.

Right there in that crumbling building Buddha's path to enlightenment was being taught. I was now living among skilled teachers and students who could support me with their advice and good example. At last I had everything I needed to take the advice from my first Buddhist book by Christmas Humphries and to

'Walk On!'

During my meditation I contemplated my own karma, beginning with life as a small child. When I was seven years old I had been sent away to La Sagesse Girls High School to become a 'young lady.' When Mary, my elder sister and I returned home after my first week in this school, Mum had met us at the front door and greeted us with the news that we had a little sister. I was shocked. Why had I not run up the stairs joyfully to meet Jean my new baby sister?

It was obviously because, at that time, my Mother was my only refuge, I did not want to share her with a new baby – and a complete stranger!

After such a difficult week in this strange new school, I wanted to be welcomed home by her with lots of hugs and kisses rather than have her turn her back on me and run up to the nursery with Mary to greet Jean. But now as Angmo introduced the idea of the Wheel of Life I realised that I myself would be born again and again and some day might find myself in the position of baby Jean. I would then surely feel more warmly towards my big sister if she came to welcome me into her world.

Angmo explained that, for as long as our minds are bound by confusion and selfishness, we are trapped in a cycle of birth, aging, sickness, death and rebirth. No one other than ourselves can free us; not even the Buddha. But as he has freed himself, he can show us all by his example and blessings how to free ourselves.

He can show us how to eliminate the deluded states of mind that bind us tightly to the Wheel of Life known as samsara.

Angmo continued, Buddha did not say that life was bad, he said that samsaric life is the nature of suffering, which is a different thing. In fact, it occurred to me that human life can occasionally be quite enjoyable, and a human life dedicated to spiritual practice would be immensely meaningful. But ordinary pleasures never last, and when our temporary good fortune ends no one has the freedom to avoid the basic sufferings of sickness, old age, death, and separation from all those we are close to.

In this life I had not starved, like many people; but I still knew suffering first hand and the prospect of re-living my life was unthinkable. How am I ever to know what my next life will bring? I could be rich, famous, live in a palace or marry a king; or I may starve to death at an early age. So I should not allow myself to be seduced by the fleeting pleasures of this life.

Yet even though I realised they would not last, out of habit I still craved friendship and comfort. But I could not bear the thought of returning to samsara for the sake of a few brief moments of pleasure. I was desperate to find real peace.

Thinking about this made it obvious I could not take refuge in anyone who had not already freed themselves from suffering. Even my own doctor can only prolong my life, not save it. He can sometimes relieve my pain, but he did not have the methods to free himself from the pain of old age, sickness and death.

I had read the life story of Buddha in *The Light of Asia* by Sir Edwin Arnold (1832 – 1904) one of the earliest translations of a Buddhist text which my postal course tutor had sent me.

Buddha Shakyamuni had been born as a prince in India and discovered the path that leads to liberation. Turning his back on his family fortune he went into the forest to meditate. Finally he attained enlightenment and dedicated the rest of his life to showing others how to do the same, sometimes performing miracles to help others and even raising people from the dead.

The time to witness miracles has long since passed,

but thanks to him, the possibility of liberating ourselves remains. Of course I am not a prince living in India in a distant time. But I found the idea of a spiritual journey very exciting. Sneaking through the jungles of my mind to find my inner enemies would be quite an adventure, but whatever I found I knew I could handle it because I was not alone. Time and distance were not obstacles to receiving blessings from the all-compassionate Buddha and I felt he would always be with me.

The spiritual path I wanted to follow is called the Dharma, and the Buddhist teachings are like a spiritual map that clearly shows the path to enlightenment and points out the pitfalls on the way. But to understand how to use the map or see how it applies to the terrain of my own mind I also needed a skilful teacher and dedicated travelling companions, who could encourage me and point out any mistaken ideas I may have. These kind spiritual friends are called 'Sangha.'

How strange it seems that all of my life the Buddha, Dharma and Sangha were there but I had not had the good fortune to know them. Even now I found some Buddhist ideas very strange as they were so different from my Catholic upbringing. But giving it a little thought I realised that Buddhism was no stranger than Christianity; I was just more familiar with Christian ideas.

Faith has an indefinable quality, an unshakable belief that goes beyond the spoken word. Perhaps faith is like love, unquantifiable. However unlike love no one can take it away.

On a trip to Durham to visit Aunty Mildred and her boys, I had first become aware of this precious jewel in the company of my cousin Paul, who was on a visit to his family from the Jesuit monastery where he lived as a priest. Paul had an aura of peace that I had never met in anyone else. I would have loved to share that peace, but the closest I got to understanding it was a ball game we played together.

Ever since then I have searched for that quiet confidence; that special aura of peace. But I had never expected to find it here in this room.

I was not yet comfortable with all of Buddha's teachings and found some ideas difficult to accept at first. One idea I had particular difficulty with is the idea of regarding everyone as my kind mother. According to Buddhist teachings we have all been reborn innumerable times and in every life we have had a mother. But where are these past mothers now? They are the people we see around us, the postman, the checkout girl, and my cat. All at some time in my innumerable past lives, have been my mother, and when they were my mother, they showed me all the kindness a mother shows her children. This is the reason Buddhists contemplate this rather strange idea: to learn to see everyone without exception as kind, for if we see someone as kind naturally we will love them.

But I found it difficult to regard even my own mother of this life as kind because she sought to ridicule and mock me at every opportunity. To her I was just a great disappointment and no matter how hard I had tried there was no way to please her. Perhaps she never understood what a challenge it was to live in a sighted world, but to be misunderstood and mistrusted by the very person that was supposed to care for me as her child made it so much harder.

So, throughout my teens I had avoided her ridicule as much as possible by hiding in my room or staying out with friends. Now I was told to regard everyone as my kind mother!

It was now time to change my mind, and until I could regard everyone as kind mothers, including my mother of this life, the doors to liberation and the

Buddhafields would remain closed. And according to the law of karma, I had the mother I deserved. Needless to say I did not overcome this gritty problem that week nor in the following months.

The issue seemed to lie heavily like a stone in my heart, but over the years my mind softened towards her and I can now view her with compassion and say perhaps she did her best, but what matters now is have I done my best.

At the end of the week's retreat Venerable Geshe Kelsang Gyatso offered to come and give a refuge ceremony for anyone interested in becoming a Buddhist. This was the moment I had longed for, the moment that I would formally become a Buddhist. After a couple of years trying to follow the Buddhist path according to my limited knowledge and ability, I would now be able to call myself a Buddhist - a follower of the Buddha. I had to improve myself to such a degree that the gap between myself and Buddha disappeared completely.

Buddha would certainly have loved my mother, so if I wanted to be like him I must learn to do the same.

The Oak Room was an unusual setting for a Buddhist ceremony. With its dark panelled walls, studded with carvings of animals and human faces, it had a sombre but very English atmosphere of brandy and cigars and the eccentric silence of a gentlemen's club. We all sat on cushions on the floor. The teacher came in and sat in front of us, also on a cushion on the floor, as did Tenzin Norbu, his translator.

The young Tibetan monk, sat on Geshe-la's right, translating into English as Geshe-la explained the meaning of the refuge ceremony and how to take refuge in the Buddha and practice Dharma; by explaining the basic refuge vows; what we had to promise to do and refrain from doing now that we were Buddhists.

The basic rules consisted of not to kill, steal or lie, to avoid sexual misconduct, and not to abuse alcohol and drugs. I was sitting about one yard from Tenzin, and as he spoke about refuge in Buddha, Dharma and Sangha, I tried to keep my mind on the words. But strange thoughts kept popping up. I was worried that Geshe Kelsang might know what I was thinking. The harder I tried to listen, the more my mind glued itself on to my strange thoughts: *Oh mind, why are you behaving so badly in front of this pure being? Why can't you concentrate on his words like everyone else?*

If I wanted to attain enlightenment I must first listen to Buddha's teachings from someone who has put this instruction into practice, someone who has actually done the work of removing their negative states of mind and cultivating positive and peaceful states. This was why I had come to Cumbria in the first place.

Finally Geshe-la explained the importance of the Sangha, the community of spiritual friends. When the ceremony was over, we were encouraged to follow the Buddhist path. Then our teacher quietly thanked us and left the room. A very simple ceremony for such an important step.

After our teacher left we went down the stairs to the dining room; but now as a group of Buddhists, Sangha brothers and sisters.

At this time life at Manjushri Institute was very basic. Most of the huge building was derelict, and its restoration would take a further twenty years of continuous work by a team of builders to complete. During the winter it was damp, cold and dark, and the living area sparsely furnished, with few warm places for residents to relax in. After a vegetarian lunch in the large communal dining room, I walked through the cloisters, my feet echoing on the cold stone tiles and into the kitchen. A few residents were gathering, and

Peter came and asked me if I would like a cup of tea before the week's community meeting. We chatted a while then went into the sitting room for the meeting. This room had no furniture except one old sofa: for the early birds. The rest of the community had to sit on cushions on the floor, while latecomers stood. Although, strictly speaking as a non-resident I was not a community member, I could now say with pride I was a Buddhist and had taken refuge in the resident teacher.

I enjoyed attending the weekly meetings, which began with the chanting of mantras and then proceeded with the week's agenda. Today at the top of the list was fund raising, followed by the Summer Fete, and the importance of closing doors to keep in the heat.

Elegina offered a bale of blanket material to make blankets from her father's factory in Italy. This was turned down as it would take too much time and effort. Her generosity rebuffed, she retorted, 'From fleas come fleas and from money comes money.' It was an Italian saying I don't quite understand.

Alice suggested bicycle repairs. This was more popular, especially when the rest of the community decided she should do it herself. After the meeting I gave her Paula's bike to begin her business and about two months later she returned it with a fresh coat of paint. This raised three pounds for the community. Perhaps these were Elegina's fleas.

I couldn't help thinking if the community had accepted her offer and made the blankets, a lot more money would have been raised, but at that time Manjushri Centre was a laidback community, with no business sense whatsoever.

However, there was quite a lot of interest in setting up craft shops and the director of Manjushri Institute had offered me the use of the old mortuary to set up a pottery, as it was surplus to the needs of the community. Almost every day I went to my icy cold pottery, but unfortunately it never succeeded in becoming more than a hobby. No matter how hard I worked, there was always some other expensive piece of equipment needed. So the Buddha images that I had imagined making in the pottery never materialised. I made little more than a few chess sets, ornaments and mugs for tourists.

On my arrival one of the residents, Chip, an American man, offered me foot therapy. I was so impressed with it, that when he organised a course in the Institute I attended and learned how to practice the techniques.

This was a wonderful way of helping others and I enjoyed the quiet space after running around all day. When he gave up his efforts to create a health centre in the damp basement I took over and organised several alternative courses. I loved the work, even though it was unpaid. But finally I had to give up with the health centre, as the damp was affecting my chest and I needed to take better care of my own health rather than spend my time removing dead rats and voles that had fallen through the hole in the skylight in this derelict part of the building. On one occasion even a little frog had found his way into the cold cellar and needed evicting. So I pushed him back through the missing pane of glass in the hatch.

One cold and dark evening, Paula came down to find me tidying up in the health centre. I asked her to close the cupboard door to conserve the heat while I finished tidying up the books inside, but before I had a chance to say, 'Don't shut the door tight!' it was closed. I immediately realised the folly of this move as there was no catch on the inside of the small cupboard door. Whatever noise we could make to attract the attention of others would be drowned out by the pounding rain. As this part of the building was derelict and all the residents were due to go into the meditation hall for prayers in a few minutes, our chances of getting out of the cupboard before breakfast were remarkably slim. What was there to help us through the night? A few health books to read and a paraffin heater which might keep us warm or kill us with its fumes. Not a pleasant prospect, so I went to the door and pushed and twisted the broken knob to no effect. Then I looked up at the skylight window which was accessible but had probably not been opened for ten years or more. The wind was howling and rain hammered on the small window, which had once been the hatch for lowering beer barrels into the cellar, probably when it was a Durham miners rest home.

I did not think that with my bare hands it would move now, so returned to the door with more determination than ever. By some good fortune the door gave way. Escaping from our small damp prison we rushed up to the meditation hall to join the rest of the community.

In the evenings Paula would often prefer to come with me to listen to the teachings rather than play with the children in the quadrangle.

Although I was frequently tired, this was the reason I had moved here and it was a great privilege to share this time with the rest of the community. This was after all our collective purpose, the reason this international group of students had come to Cumbria. Every day about seventy people waited expectantly in the meditation hall, all eyes focused on the open door, for the arrival of our precious teacher. Tenzin, his translator, would carry the sacred texts and then translate Geshe-la's commentary for us, as we scratched down the words in our notepads in English. Most of the instructions we heard then are now in print, having been carefully transcribed, edited and published. Indeed, these days, many of the instructions are not only in paper book form but are also available as CDs, making them accessible even to me.

Manjushri Institute was first established in nineteen seventy-six when the Buddhist community purchased the vast crumbling property of Conishead Priory.

Lama Yeshe had been touring all over the world for several years, giving courses on Tibetan Buddhism to hundreds of dedicated students. He saw that what was needed was a more permanent base in the West which would function as a kind of Buddhist College. When a wealthy Swiss lady called Sigrid, asked how she could help, he suggested she use her money to buy a building in England that could become the first major Buddhist Centre of the Gelug tradition. Some of Lama Yeshe's Western students, looked around for a suitable property and eventually chose this grade-two listed building, with its leaking roof and galloping dry rot, which they felt would be ideal for a Buddhist Community.

After a short course, in the summer of nineteen seventy-seven given by Lama Yeshe to inaugurate the Centre, which sadly I could not attend due to lack of funds, Venerable Geshe Kelsang had been invited to live here as the resident teacher.

With Geshe-la's arrival that year, teachings could be held continuously, and Buddhism began to flourish in Cumbria. Visitors flocked to Manjushri Institute in ever increasing numbers to attend courses, which attracted many students from all over the world.

The following year, Venerable. Geshe Kelsang created a new Buddhist centre in York and since then the movement has spread worldwide. But in those early days Manjushri Institute was still a ruin and the 'health centre' was a real health hazard.

The damp, sunless basement was no place to be,

either during summer or winter. Many things have changed since the early days. But one thing has not changed: the reason for visiting. People come not for the comfort of their bodies, but to heal their minds.

After the evening's instruction Paula and I went down for supper of soup and toast before the puja or chanted meditation. Washing up done, it was now time to rush back up the stairs to the meditation hall for chanting and prayers.

Twice a month there was a special group meditation which included making extensive offerings. It was similar to a cross between a harvest festival and a Catholic Mass. All afternoon people had been working in the kitchen as volunteer cooks and wonderful smells were wafting up the kitchen stairs. Now these kind people were taking the food into the meditation room and arranging it in front of the shrine to be offered to the Buddhas.

During the ceremony, the blessed food was given out as the participants sang praises. I was never able to take part in the preparation and distribution of the food, but I could still rejoice in the hard work of these kind volunteers.

When the crowds dispersed the forgotten army of dish-washers and cleaners moved in and put everything back in place. At that time the Tibetan tradition was followed as closely as possible, and an approximation of Tibetan tea was served on these occasions. The smoky taste of Lapsang Souchong simulated the flavour produced by the traditional wood fire, and then generous quantities of milk, butter and salt were added and blended to make a wonderful creamy drink. The first time I tried it, it was quite a shock, as it tasted more like chicken soup than tea, but it soon became my favourite drink and I looked forward eagerly to these special occasions. As a source of energy and warmth it is unequalled. It was not difficult to see why the Tibetans loved it in their mountain snows.

As I had discovered during my first visit to Conishead Priory in February nineteen seventy-nine, there were showers in the basement, but only for the brave. A brown piece of cardboard torn from a cardboard packing box indicated in red marker pen if a man or woman was in the showers at that time. The most likely occupant, however, would be a rat.

After undressing in a damp, disused bathroom, it was necessary to run across the corridor naked to the shower, which had no door or curtain. There was nowhere to hang a towel. But once the water flowed, it was a wonderful source of heat in an otherwise freezing building. These showers had been installed for the previous occupants of the building who no doubt had unlimited central heating as they were from the Durham mines and were here for the benefit of their health. I had used this facility once or twice and came out cold but clean, but it was not long before I discovered the delights of a shower on the first floor, hardly luxurious by most people's standards but an improvement on the basement. I was lucky not to have to live in this cold old building, and was glad to get back to my flat with a bathroom and hot running water. But returning to the flat every night, in the damp, cold weather sapped my strength, even though it was just a short walk.

Paula said that she wanted to be a Buddhist. As it was usually only adults who took refuge, she got special permission from Geshe Kelsang to join a group of adults in his room for the ceremony, the same one that I had taken in the Oak Room the previous year. That evening I walked home with Kelsang Tsering, the smallest Buddhist in town. Geshe Kelsang had kindly given her this name.

Each evening the resident teacher, Venerable Geshe Kelsang Gyatso, gave us instruction from one of the classic Tibetan texts. Day after day, he patiently explained the meaning of the text while the group of about seventy disciples and visitors sat on the floor on small cushions, taking notes.

Although I was still struggling to understand Tenzin's Tibetan accent and some of the terminology was very obscure, there was an aura of love and closeness in the room which I had never experienced before. The meaning I had been searching for all these years was somewhere in that room and I hoped that it might reveal itself to me some day, until then I had to be satisfied that I was fortunate enough to be a part of it.

Most of the students had spent time in India and some had even learned to speak Tibetan. Our Tibetan lessons took place in the large dining room throughout the winter. About ten of us huddled around the stove as Samten, another of the Tibetan translators, taught us basic Tibetan. When I asked him if they had grammar text books, he seemed very puzzled and didn't understand what I meant. Even if they had existed, I doubt I would have understood them anyway as I had not understood the French grammar taught by sister Cecelia when I was fourteen, but Samten the gentle Tibetan monk would *not* have slapped my face for this.

At this time all the prayers we chanted together were in Tibetan, but were transcribed into Roman script in our prayer books so that those who could not read Tibetan script could join in with the chanting. A rough translation of each verse was found on the right hand side of the Tibetan phonetics, and at the back of the prayer book the whole text could be found written in the Tibetan script, for the Tibetans and anyone else who could read Tibetan. In the sitting room I met Jill, a nurse who had learned to speak Tibetan when travelling in India. When she noticed me looking at a prayer book she explained to me in a shy, quiet voice why the prayer books were presented in such a complicated way. She said, 'It is important to include the original Tibetan, in case there were mistakes in the rough translations or in the Roman transcription of the Tibetan; the meaning would then have been lost forever.' Then she said that until there was someone who had a deep enough understanding of the meaning of the text, it would not be possible for us to make authentic translations from Tibetan into English or any other Western language, but at this time there were no Westerners with a profound understanding of Tibetan or of Buddhism, and there were no Tibetan Masters with a thorough command of any western language. Thirty years later things have changed a lot and these days the same texts have been properly translated into several western languages and rough translations and phonetics are a thing of the past. But many of us who were around in the early days remember the pujas (chanted prayers and meditations) with nostalgia. Although I understood very little of what we were singing, their sound had a profound effect on me. The Tibetan tunes were hauntingly beautiful; charged with a mystical power which transmitted the blessings of so many great Lamas who had chanted them over the centuries.

I took part in anything I could - pujas, guided meditations, short retreats or teachings, and the more I did the more I enjoyed.

Often Paula and I went to the Centre for the daily seven o'clock Manjushri puja. On bright sunny summer mornings it was a lovely way to start the day, passing the string of race horses going for their morning exercise on the beach as we made our way to the

Priory. But during the winter months it was a different story as we walked along the cold, unlit lanes to the front door. For me at the time there seemed no better way to start the day than with this short meditation on the Wisdom Buddha, thereby inviting the energy of wisdom into my daily life. Paula would often beg me to wake her early so that she could attend the puja before she set off to school on the bus with the other children.

During morning meditation in the winter most of the participants sat wrapped in army surplus blankets to keep out the damp and cold, indeed the building was so cold that many people wore these blankets all day long.

Manjushri is the Buddha of Wisdom. In Buddhism, wisdom and compassion are seen as equally important and are often compared to the two wings of a bird. Just as a bird needs both wings to fly, we need to develop both wisdom and compassion if we are to fly to enlightenment. Connecting with the Buddha of Wisdom every morning was the most wonderful way of starting the day.

Many different Buddhas are visualised and worshipped in the faith, but they should not be regarded as being like different gods.

Manjushri is the Buddha of Wisdom and is represented as wielding a sword to cut through our ignorance, and Avalokiteshvara, the Buddha of Compassion, is depicted as having a thousand arms with which to help all living beings.

But Manjushri and Avalokiteshvara are not different people. Manjushri is the symbolic embodiment of the wisdom of the universal enlightened mind, while Avalokiteshvara is the embodiment of the compassion of the same enlightened mind. By praying to and meditating on Manjushri, we connect with universal wisdom and awaken our own wisdom, and by praying to Avalokiteshvara we connect with universal compassion and awaken our own compassion.

Traditionally in Buddhism the day is divided into two parts, the meditation session and the meditation break. Both parts are equally important, though generally we spend much more time engaged in daily activities than sitting on our meditation cushion. However, it is vitally important that we spend at least a little time every day meditating. The purpose of meditation is to cultivate peaceful and positive states of mind. Starting the day with just twenty minutes soaking our mind in love, compassion, wisdom, equanimity or any other positive state, will carry over into our daily life and enable us to transform everyday activities into the spiritual path.

I found Jill again in the Priory sitting room waiting for a friend and asked her about the Buddhist Path, 'How is it possible to become a Buddha if you are always busy doing other things?' She explained that a pure Buddhist must watch their mind in all situations. Or at least in my case try to. She said that one famous text advises, 'When alone watch your mind. When with others watch your speech.' Good advice for anyone, Buddhist or non Buddhist, but in my experience easier to say than do, as habits are hard to break. I was aware from my reading that the best motivation is to work for the benefit of others and to look at any situation from the point of view of the other person. Perhaps Mrs Duffy, my last teacher in La Sagesse junior school, had been a Buddhist in a past life!

Whenever I think of her she always comes to mind as a shining example.

Jill, who like me was brought up as a Catholic, said the main difference between Catholicism and Buddhism, is that although Buddhas have miraculous powers, there is one thing they cannot do. They cannot save suffering beings in the way that a mother cat saves her kittens from danger by picking them up by the scruff of their neck, with no effort on their part. All a Buddha can do is to show us the way to free ourselves from suffering. After that it is up to us to do the necessary work on our minds, and thereby free ourselves. Buddhas can help us with this work by arranging favourable conditions, but they cannot do the work for us, nor can they make us do it.

When I was a Catholic, the responsibility seemed to lie more with Jesus Christ who died on the cross to atone for our sins, thus enabling us to enter Heaven and be saved, but I was now being told that the Buddhas cannot enlighten anyone. We came into this life with what we deserve, we get what we deserve and when we leave this life we will take with us what we deserve. This made more sense to me than the idea of a saviour. Now David, Jill's friend, came in and sat down with us. David had also travelled in India and they described their time in Dharamsala with the Tibetans. Although they had gone to India to become yoga teachers, they soon found that the Tibetan teaching on karma and rebirth held more substance for them.

So simple and so logical was the description of karma, that they wondered why they had not found it before. At its simplest it is just cause and effect. You reap what you sow, but karma cannot work without the belief in rebirth. No two people come into this world equal, they come to live a unique life faced with unique experiences and with their own unique good or bad luck. But their good and bad luck has been created by themselves in their past lives and brought forward into this life as potential for pleasant or unpleasant experiences. According to the way they live this life they will leave with a whole new set of imprints. David's description of karma made a deep impression on me.

At first I found this idea difficult to accept. How could I have created the cause for so much suffering in my early life? I had often felt misunderstood and unfairly treated; there could be no greater misunderstanding than to be raped by someone who thought that he was doing me a good turn. I stayed angry for many years, wishing that he would suffer. But I could not think of a punishment bad enough for him.

Did I really now have to accept the responsibility for being raped? Some day I would have to forgive him. But perhaps I would leave this for a future meditation and instead deal with some smaller resentments. Should I forgive my sister Mary for poisoning me with lupin seeds? Yes, and I had already forgiven her; it was not difficult as she was very young and, although she knew it was a naughty thing to do, she would not have realised how serious the outcome might have been.

I am sure she had not intended to kill me. So having forgiven Mary I could now go through my life during my meditation sessions, forgiving one by one all those who I felt had hurt me. Bad memories are similar to those poisonous lupin seeds. Normally when they surface they poison my mind, as they did whenever I recalled my mother's frequent anger towards me. But I discovered that if, when these memories arose, I looked at her with complete acceptance and compassion these same memories became like powerful medicine to heal my mind. I could become like a wolf that can eat lupin seeds with no ill effect!

I heard Jill talking quietly to David, saying that she was planning to change her life from fulfilling her own selfish desires to a life of caring for others. I asked her why she thought she needed to change as she was a nurse and to my mind she was already caring for others. She replied, 'Yes, I am a nurse and already care for others but my attitude to caring for those others would be much better if I applied my Buddhist beliefs and did not forget my motivation to care for everyone equally. In the future I will try and look at the needs of the patients from their point of view, rather than from my own. This way of thinking is very much encouraged in our Buddhist tradition and protects us from acting selfishly.'

I had just become a Buddhist, a follower of the

Buddha. The Buddha can be thought of as the Doctor. I had taken refuge in Dharma, the instructions that Buddha taught and which are still relevant today.

This can be thought of as the medicine that the Buddha has prescribed to heal my mind; and I had taken refuge in Sangha, the spiritual community, not just the monks and nuns but anyone who followed the Buddhist path purely. These could be compared to the nurses like Jill who care for sick people. Seeing how my mind held onto so much resentment, and ignorant of how to cure myself, I could hardly deny that I was sick. But David and Jill were real Sangha friends, they had shown me so much about the power of meditation. I had seen what good people they were and I certainly wanted to become like them.

Next time I saw Jill she said how much her life had changed and how so many of her problems had been resolved simply by watching her own mind, instead of projecting her problems onto the external situation. She explained: 'Normally, we think our problems exist out there, in the material world or in how others are treating us, so we feel that the solution must be to change the world and other people.' But Jill now felt that she had discovered that the real problem was in her own mind, and so by changing her mental attitude she could actually solve her own inner problems. 'This is the real source of happiness!' she exclaimed. She had been very excited at the prospect of visiting again and spending some quiet time reflecting on her progress as a Buddhist; taking the opportunity to go on quiet woodland walks and share in the group meditations. Seeing how much change she had made, I hoped that I had also changed since I last saw her.

Continuing our discussion we agreed that not only do we feel that our problems exist out there; we also feel that our happiness can be found out there too.

That is how I often view my own life. It is like an eternal itch that won't go away. Most of my time is wasted in dreaming of an illusive future happiness; rather than recognising that happiness can be in the present moment. If I could change my thinking patterns, instead of dreaming about what was; or what might be. Jill said she now recognised this way of thinking was nonsense. We have already had so many of the things we thought would make us happy, and maybe they did – but for a short while only. Sooner or later problems always recur. The same occurs with the places we live in, with our partners – with everything. We tend to envy the rich and successful, those who can fulfil most of their desires. But we only have to read magazines about the rich and famous to see that wealth and glamour often bring greater suffering.

'Yes, of course we know this,' Jill said, 'but out of habit we keep looking outside ourselves for happiness, only to be disappointed time and time again.'

This sounded so familiar to me, and I remembered my own quest for happiness: when I moved to Cornwall to visit my father who I had not seen for many years. I went there looking for happiness. Not finding real happiness in his small village, I moved to Devon to work in Plymouth. I found a job in shop display that I loved but still I had problems as the money was not enough to live on. So I moved back to Hastings to be near my mother where I had to take a hotel job which was better paid, but gave less satisfaction. Finding no real happiness on the South Coast I returned to Newcastle again.

Still seeking illusive happiness, I continued to search, sometimes in relationships, at other times in my art; but the haunting search continued unfulfilled until I came here and found the path to freedom from suffering. Of course having found the path is not the same as saying that I have walked it, I have simply got the map. But at least I now know that happiness is just a state of mind, and so if I want to be happy all the time what I need to do is work on my mind rather than change my external conditions.

Chapter 3

THE BODHISATTVA PATH

The Buddha is a rainbow composed of every hue
My friend is sunshine yellow and my enemy dark
blue
But if I can work hard enough with yellow, green
and blue
I may one day be good enough to be a Buddha too.

Sometimes I felt like a sculptor, carving away the stone to reveal a new mind. As I chipped away at my mind, it gradually began to take on a different shape revealing a new and more beautiful appearance, one with a calm and peaceful expression, soft curves and gentle manner. Not the rough and craggy rock that was there at the beginning. But there is always room for improvement on this invisible sculpture, and I hope that it will eventually resemble a pure Buddha,

I had considered myself a Buddhist for a couple of years but in reality I was just beginning my spiritual journey. When I took part in the refuge ceremony I formally became a Buddhist and was told how to liberate myself from all of my future suffering. The next step was to take the Bodhisattva vows. But what are these? I was told that a Bodhisattva is someone who has made a promise to dedicate their whole life to the attainment of enlightenment and become a pure Buddha.

To do this I needed to familiarise myself with the moral discipline of a practising Buddhist. I could never become a Bodhisattva until I gave up even the smallest intention to harm another person, and in future all of my actions of body, speech and mind would have to be performed with this intention. Moral discipline is the cornerstone of any Buddhist practice and little by little I would need to familiarise myself with the minds of love and compassion of a Bodhisattva.

Having listened to my teacher, now I understood that the root of most of my problems was in my past lives. This was the simple law of cause and effect, or karma. In this life I could only experience what I myself had created the cause for. According to Buddhism, all of us created the cause for our present living conditions long before we were born. Why did I need to know this? Because with this knowledge I could begin to live according to the law of karma.

Now I saw clearly how my prayer to have something to replace my painting had been answered. I had been given a new set of paints: stronger, brighter and more vivid than any I had seen before. And I had also been given a blank canvas, the canvas of my mind.

But how could I paint the future? Through meditation.

When I saw my enemy in my mind's eye, what I needed to do was paint him with a beautiful smiling expression wearing wonderful clothes and hope that all of his wishes for happiness are fulfilled. I could paint happiness and I could paint joy. In time I would even learn to paint my enemies as special friends. And every day I could paint the images of Buddhas in my mind. In a mind filled with these pure images there would be no space for anger or sadness. And over the years I could add everyone I had ever met. No matter what happens outside my own mind I now had the power to paint it beautiful.

If I hadn't seen my life was the nature of suffering, I would not have had the wish to liberate myself from it.

I could now empathise with everyone else who was

trapped in a life of pain and guilt. Empathy gives rise to compassion, and compassion finally leads to the determination to actually do something to help free others from suffering. From a Buddhist point of view, it is not enough just to help relieve a few people from hunger or thirst. What a bodhisattva needs to do is to free all beings from all of their suffering by leading them to Nirvana.

But how can I possibly free all beings from suffering? What an outrageously ambitious idea!

I don't even know how to free myself from suffering, so of course it is impossible to free anyone else. The only person who can do this is a Buddha, someone who has completely eradicated all their own faults and limitations and developed infinite compassion, wisdom and spiritual power. So now I know if I wish to help others, I need to become a Buddha. The wish to become a Buddha in order to help all living beings is called Bodhichitta, a Sanskrit word meaning 'mind of enlightenment.' Someone who has Bodhichitta is called a Bodhisattva: an awakening being.

The Bodhisattva's way of life is based on putting the needs of the other person first; I have heard it said that if someone was to steal from me or even take my partner, my reaction to this should be to rejoice in their happiness. Why should I rejoice in what everyone would call my misfortune? This is a very uncommon mindset to develop. But this unusual attitude will actually benefit me. How?

If I can have a loving mind towards those who cause me harm and not just towards those who please me, my mind will remain calm and peaceful all the time.

How exciting life was becoming now.

I was being shown how to gain some real control over my mind. Of course there was still a long way to go, but what mattered was I had finally begun to make sense of my past. If I had been happier in my teens and had less problems during my school days I would not have sought to find the root of these problems. Nor would I have developed any interest in the Buddhist path, which starts with the realisation that the human condition is one of suffering. This is the first of the four Noble Truths common to all Buddhist traditions: True suffering; true origins; true cessations and true paths. Of course there had been happy times in my life but I was not a stranger to suffering and wanted to know how to avoid it.

I had been brought up to believe that I should be happy. Children expressing anything but a pleasing disposition were punished, while happy and contented children were praised and rewarded.

But I had not forgotten little Philippa imprisoned in her cot, cold and hungry while the rest of the family ate breakfast in front of the warm kitchen fire. How many times since then had I experienced cold, hunger and loneliness? I was supposed to have been a happy child, but the reality was that often I was anything but happy. Buddha's declaration that our life is the nature of suffering made much more sense to me. This, after all had been my experience so far. If I was the only person that suffered this would not be such a big problem. But my mother had suffered unbearable sadness, and had no way of finding peace. My father had experienced years of mental torment and I had been powerless to help either of them.

I had already taken refuge in the Buddha to protect myself from suffering. But now I was about to take the Bodhisattva vow, a promise to help all others who were experiencing much greater suffering than me.

As long as I could recall I had been uneasy with the stereotyped idea of a happy life and had never fitted the mould.

Now I could break out of the mould! There is something rather shallow about this superficial happiness; the happiness we experience when things are going well is just a distraction from our underlying pain. If our happiness only depends on external conditions – like having a well paid job, a nice house, good health or some alcohol or drugs to remove the pain, then what will happen when these conditions change?

I was very excited because now Geshe-la was going to grant the Bodhisattva Vows to anyone who was interested. Traditionally this is taken in front of a Spiritual Guide by means of a simple ceremony. Ten years earlier it would not have been possible to receive these vows without travelling to India.

There was great excitement in the room and all eyes were on the door as we waited expectantly for the teacher to enter.

The room was full and some of the students were whispering nervously together, while others muttered mantras quietly to themselves. Some of the students, who had been to India, had already received these vows from other Lamas. I had not, but remembered when I had my first private interview with Geshe-la he had simply said, 'You should think of others.'

Such easy advice, but the best I had ever received. Time and time again, while thinking of the needs of others my own problems have faded away and this has proved to be a real source of happiness.

Geshe-la began by explaining the six perfections: giving, moral discipline, patience, effort, mental stabilisation and wisdom.

Of course we all give gifts to our friends and relatives from time to time, but the idea of giving fearlessness was new to me. Protecting others from fear must indeed be a form of giving, and he explained how easy it is to gain some merit by freeing insects from danger when they are drowning in water. This, I believe, is particularly important for a person like me who has delighted in harming small helpless insects in the past.

Then he described the second perfection, which was moral discipline, without which our life would become chaotic and we might act out all of our impulsive desires without taking into account the feelings of others.

Pausing a moment to think before we act would prevent many problems for ourselves and others. How much suffering is caused by mindless behaviour, by acting without thinking how it will affect others.

When I was raped as a teenager, this mindless act affected me dramatically thereafter, and led to many years of hatred for the man, but actually I got off lightly. Many women are raped in far more brutal ways, or even killed. According to the law of karma my rapist will suffer unimaginably in future lives, so now I know that there is no need for me to retaliate. My feelings of resentment are like poison which can only serve to harm me. If someone offered me a poisonous drink would I choose to drink it? My own anger is like poison for my mind and instead of dwelling on that anger, I need to feel compassion for him and for everyone else who is involved in rape, not just for the victim but also for the aggressor.

Accepting harm and suffering without feeling angry or upset is the third perfection, the perfection of patience. We definitely need a lot of patience to live peacefully in this chaotic world. The next three vows – effort, mental stabilisation and wisdom - are mainly practiced during our meditation.

When the ceremony was over, I had a slight

headache from the concentration and a mixture of feeling elevated and exhausted all at the same time. It was as if I had now been born as a baby Bodhisattva. But would I ever be good enough to be a Buddha? Had I not behaved too badly in the past? And did it matter if I had forgotten most of my bad actions in this life? There were so many questions, but there must be answers.

So I asked Jill what she thought as she had already taken these vows in India. Reassuringly she said that listing my past bad actions was not the point of taking these vows.

'We cannot change the past but we can influence the future. By practising the moral discipline of a Bodhisattva right now our past wrong deeds will gradually be purified.'

Having taken the vows I needed to change my way of thinking, but no one expected me to be perfect.

As Geshe-la explained, we had only promised to keep them to the best of our ability. No skill is attained without repeated effort; every tennis player or top golfer begins in the same way, gradually practising until they perfect their sport. So it is with Buddhism.

Taking these vows in front of my Spiritual Guide for the first time was a very special moment that I will never forget. It marked the start of the Bodhisattva's way of life – the path to enlightenment. The refuge vows I had previously taken were designed to protect me from suffering in this and future lives, but the Bodhisattva vows were there to enable me finally to become a protector of all living beings.

While waiting in the queue for lunch I asked my friend Margaret how we could practice the Bodhisattva vows in our daily life. After reflecting for a few moments she replied, 'For me what works best is to practice equanimity. I am trying to develop an equal friendliness towards everyone, free from the biased emotions of anger, attachment and indifference.'

This led us into a conversation about anger. I said I felt we usually think another person makes us angry; we feel it is their fault and it is almost as if our anger came from them. After all, in everyday conversation we would normally say, 'He made me angry,' rather than, 'When I saw him anger arose in my mind.'

But Margaret insisted, 'My anger does arise from my own mind. Another person might trigger off my anger but they cannot produce it. So if I don't wish to experience anger I have to find a method to evict it. Since anger resides in my own mind and not in any external circumstances, I alone am responsible for it and all the consequences of letting it fly out of my mind. Though anger lives in my mind, it is not a part of it – it is more like an unpleasant tenant I have foolishly allowed to live in the house of my mind. When I see that all this tenant does is cause trouble, hurting both myself and others, I am free to evict him. This of course takes time, for he will not be willing to go, but as long as my determination does not waver and I practice diligently, eventually I will force him to leave.'

'That sounds about right, Margaret. But what will I do if I have no anger? Will people abuse me?'

'Maybe they will, but not because you have no anger. They will abuse you if you have already created the karmic cause for them to do so – through getting angry yourself and abusing others in the past.'

'So if I react with anger now, I shall have to return and face the consequences in this, or a future life?'

'Worse still, the ripples of even a small bit of anger will grow and grow until it is repaid. It is a debt that must be repaid, either right now or in the future.'

'By not reacting to abuse I will purify my original action, as a result I will harm neither myself nor others.

This way I will be happy now and in future lives?'

These ideas are not new in our western culture. My favourite poet is William Blake and my favourite poem has the lines:

> *'I was angry with my friend:*
> *I told my wrath, my wrath did end.*
> *I was angry with my foe;*
> *I told him not, my wrath did grow...'*

There must be countless other examples in our literature.

As we sat by the dining room window eating our lunch, we continued our discussion.

Margaret said, 'Attachment is a bigger problem than anger. As a result of allowing the seductively beautiful hummingbird of attachment to stay in my mind I have performed countless negative actions in the past. Worse still, if I don't evict this bird right now, it will continue to dictate my behaviour, causing unimaginable suffering for myself and others, right now and in future lives. Like anger, attachment is not a part of my mind but more like an uninvited guest who is certainly not planning to leave.

'Anger is a rough and bad mannered guest, so it is easy to recognise him and see what he's up to. But attachment is subtle and smooth talking. She creeps softly and quietly in to your mind almost unnoticed. She pretends to be your friend. She pretends to be love. So we have to be very observant. We need to evict attachment but allow love to stay in our heart.'

Now I asked her, 'How do you tell love and attachment apart? Though at first they may look similar, in reality they are completely different. Attachment is a delusion and causes no end of pain. Whereas pure, selfless love never causes problems, neither for myself nor others. Attachment seems to be our friend. She whispers in our ear, "Follow me, I will make you happy. I will lead you to the sweetest flowers." But if we follow her we will waste our life. We will fly from flower to flower, from distraction to distraction, but we will never find any nectar that can quench our thirst for happiness. This way we become like a child's balloon, blown hither and thither from one meaningless, momentary pleasure to another, never finding what we are really looking for.'

I was reminded of another of my favourite poets, T.S. Eliot:

> 'Distracted from distraction by distraction
> Filled with fancies and empty of meaning ...
> Men and bits of paper,
> Whirled by the cold wind ...'

The desires of attachment are never satiated, and following them always produces more desires. Until I get the object of my desire my mind is restless, hungry, in pain. But if I succeed in obtaining it, then immediately there is the problem of making it last. If I lose it, I am filled with grief. And if I do not, I get bored and new desires come to take its place. At no stage is there peace or satisfaction.

Margaret went to the kitchen to make us tea while I pondered our discussion. On her return she told me about her family then we went to the shop to buy some books. After that, I went for a woodland walk. In spite of the cloudy sky, this was a day to remember. I had attended the ceremony this morning and entered the Bodhisattva path, becoming a Mahayana Buddhist. If I continue on this path till the end I will become a Buddha and will be able to repay the kindness of everyone, for everyone without exception has helped in so many ways in the past. Even those who have harmed me and whom I currently dislike, have in fact in some previous life helped me greatly, so I must rid myself of the falsely discriminating mind that divides people into friends, enemies and strangers, and determine to repay the kindness of everyone without exception, irrespective of how they are treating me at the moment.

Until I achieve full enlightenment, there will be many occasions on which I must accept help from others. As a blind person, much of my time is lived with the help of kind people and I sometimes wonder how much merit I use up by having the assistance of so many people, when I feel I have so little to offer them in return. Of course when I become a Buddha I can help all of them, but meanwhile there must be many small ways to help others if I seek them. Having a disability is not an excuse for laziness or selfishness but a wonderful opportunity to practice patience. Even if I cannot help physically, I can always lend a patient and understanding ear, say a kind word, or send out loving thoughts and prayers. Not only that; if someone offers to help me and I accept their help it could be said I am giving them the opportunity to practice giving. After all it would not be possible to give unless there was someone to receive the help. So with the right attitude my actions can be virtuous all the time and even accepting help can be a way of giving.

As a Bodhisattva I need to develop the wish to help all beings, but how can I do this when I don't know them all? I will have to start by overcoming the delusions in my own mind. As this may take many lives I should begin this practice to the best of my ability right now. The first step might be to pray to my Guru and the Three Jewels to bless me with the courage to work on my mind regardless of the hardships I meet. And as every disabled person knows hardship is no stranger. Our friends and family may mean well but often swing from over protection to a lack of support when it is needed most.

So disabled people have extra opportunities to develop patience, not only with their own bodies, but also with those around them who occasionally make life more difficult while trying to help.

But a disability should never be an excuse to avoid helping others. And at the moment I can still see quite well, my problems only arise when I move about in unfamiliar places. If I remain open to helping others then when the opportunity arises, I will recognise it. Sometimes simply going about my daily life without complaining may be an inspiration to others. And the truth is that all people are to some degree disabled, because although they may have mastered worldly skills, they do not know how to control the problems that arise in their own minds.

Uplifted by the day's events I went back inside as rain began to fall and I was getting rather wet. Finding Margaret again, we resumed our conversation on equanimity.

'Margaret, what bothers me is that if we get rid of the minds of hatred and attachment, surely we will only be left with an indifferent feeling towards everyone?'

'This is certainly not the point of meditating on equanimity. Indifference is just as deluded and self-centred as hatred and attachment. We feel indifferent towards someone who stimulates within us neither feelings of pleasure nor displeasure. If our only basis for relating to someone is how they make us feel, then it is true that getting rid of the emotions of hatred and attachment would leave us with indifference.

'But the point of meditation on equanimity is to provide us with a non self-centred basis for relating to others. If we reflect on how the essential wish of each and every living being is to be happy and not to suffer, we will come to empathise with them as individuals in their own right, And if we remember that all of us live together in the same world and are totally dependent upon one another, we will come to feel close to them and develop a sense of gratitude.

'Since everyone without exception has the same basic wishes, possesses Buddha Nature, and is part of the web of interdependence, then through meditating on these points over and over again, gradually we will develop a feeling of equal friendliness towards all living beings, irrespective of how they are making us feel at the moment. This is equanimity.'

I asked Margaret, 'Why is equanimity so important?'

'It is the basis of true love and true compassion. At the moment, when a friend or relative is suffering, we feel compassion for them and wish to help them. This is good, but generally it is not pure compassion because it is mixed with attachment. In part at least, we want to help them because their pain makes *us* feel bad. Our wish to help is therefore more about us than about them. This kind of emotional compassion has little power to help and can even cause us suffering.

'Compassion based on equanimity is not emotional, but has the clear, calm and impersonal quality of wisdom. It has immense power and never causes suffering. Wisdom and compassion are the two wings of Buddhist practice. Compassion without wisdom can be over emotional and rather stupid, while wisdom without compassion can be cold, calculating and filled with pride. But when compassion and wisdom are united together, we will be of real service to others. We will be like an eagle that can fly high in the sky; we can lift others out of their mundane problems and show them the path to happiness.'

The questions ended when Margaret had to return to work in the kitchen. I sat on and contemplated our discussion a while before going to the office to pay my bill. I loved the office as Peter was always fun to talk to. He often disapproved of my flippant responses, but he was a real friend, always there when needed, often even before I thought I needed his help.

Such friends are rare treasures. Perhaps I had less money than most people, but material things are never enough anyhow. What matters is a mind satisfied with these few possessions. I was content with what I had, as long as I could pay my bill in the office and buy enough to eat. If I could do that, I felt I was rich.

Little by little I sorted through the nooks and crannies of my mind, tidying up the junk in my inner attics and cellars, sweeping them clean during my meditation. This was a very joyful time. Having cleared a little space in my mind I now tried to put my new Bodhisattva vows into neat compartments.

Tibet's misfortune was our good fortune. In fact my teacher's name 'Kelsang' means good fortune. 'Gyatso' means 'ocean.' Now this Ocean of Good Fortune lived right here in Ulverston, only ten minutes from my door. This was fortune beyond my wildest dreams! No need to travel to India any more. I have a great sage living next door.

Peter met me on the stairs and he walked to the front door with me as we discussed the day's events. Peter had a calm peaceful manner and was always to be found doing what others did not wish to do. His unobtrusive kindness and quiet way were perhaps hiding a great man, one well on the way along the Bodhisattva path. I applied some lipsalve, and Peter asked if I knew what the parrot had said to the shopkeeper when he went to a pharmacy for some lipsalve? Of course as usual I did not know the answer.

Peter said, when the shopkeeper asked how he wished to pay the parrot replied, 'Just put it on my bill.'

That was pure Peter.

And whenever I needed Peter he was there. I hope some of that selfless love will rub off on me. It is very important who we have as friends. If we have good friends we are more likely to behave well than if we have friends who are a bad influence. Peter was certainly a special friend.

On the quiet walk back home to my flat that evening I took stock of the day. Then I took stock of my life. As a tiny baby I had wanted my mother to hold me in her arms and hug me tightly; as a child I sought to please her but seemed only to cause her grief; as a teenager I had kept my distance.

This brought back memories of my art college days where I had found the warmth and friendship that I craved for in the arms of Barry. Having just left a girl's boarding school all of my previous friendships had been with girls not boys. So I lacked confidence or social skill when communicating with boys.

I recalled my feeling of being close to him; this had been at once strange and exciting. I continued to think about what attracted me to him, and although many years had passed he still held some special place in my mind.

Then I turned my attention to the night that I went to a party and found him in the arms of Marian, who during our school days had been one of my best friends. I was inconsolable at the pain; the sense of loss. Soon after that my friend Jancie introduced me to a good friend of hers to cheer me up. I don't know how she thought a person such as that would have ever cheered me up: with little personality, charm or even some level of dress sense. I did not feel cheered up at all. So I went upstairs alone to get away from him but he followed me up and, through a combination of my lack of experience in communicating with strange young men and my indifference to this one, he misunderstood my body language and out of ignorance raped me.

It is not difficult to recreate the pain that my relationship with Marian and these two young men brought and in my imagination I could still relive the feelings that I had experienced so many years ago. What an irony to lose a boyfriend that I was very fond of because I wanted to remain a virgin and then the following week (yes, the following week) to be raped by someone who thought I was missing sex, and who presumably had not realised my friendship with Barry was based on our shared interest in art, not sex.

During my meditation I could picture both men clearly in my mind's eye as if it was today.

All the emotions that had accompanied this painful experience were lit up in my mind again. Now I was being told I had to love everyone equally. But was my mind a waste disposal unit? Would it be possible to reabsorb the pain that had after all arisen in my mind and dissolve it by developing a mind of universal love? Perhaps like an alchemist I could transform the pain into a mind of equanimity? How wonderful *that* mind would be!

And having come to this conclusion I sat down quietly on my meditation cushion before my altar. Gently closing my eyes I sat and watched my breath moving softly in and out. I was aware of the room and the sensation at the tip of my nose as I observed the warm breath entering and leaving my body. When my mind became calm and relaxed, I focused on Peter my helpful and kind friend, aware of the comfort of his friendship and support. Then I turned my attention to Fred, the man who had raped me; I could feel the tension rising in my body and mind at the memory, which had not faded over the passage of time. After that I focused on a lady who had passed me in the street and felt a little more relaxed again. This woman had neither harmed me nor helped me; she was just a passer-by.

Again I focused on Peter. Why did I like him? Obviously because he liked me: he made me feel good. Why did I dislike Fred? Because he made me feel bad. And why was I indifferent to the lady in the street? Because she neither stimulated feelings of pleasure nor displeasure.

So my division of people into friends, enemies and strangers boiled down simply to how they made me feel: to my emotions. But feelings are fickle and subjective. Tomorrow Peter might do something that upsets me and make me feel bad. Fred could come back into my life and we could get over the past and become friends. And I could have a pleasant or unpleasant encounter with the lady in the street leading to friendship or animosity. But there are surely people who dislike Peter; he is an enemy as well as a friend. Fred must have relatives and friends who love him. And the lady in the street is not a stranger to everyone. So the categories of friend, enemy and stranger are not as fixed and clearly defined as I had thought. Surely there is a better way of relating to people than solely on the basis of how they make me - and only me – feel at any given moment.

One thing we all have in common is the wish to be happy and avoid suffering. That is what made me come here and take the Bodhisattva vows. Now I am told the pathway to eternal happiness is by dedicating my whole life to the happiness of others.

Over the months I returned to this meditation again and again and gradually my rigid mind became less defensive. The fear of hurt and rejection dissolved away and my fear was replaced by a new openness, a willingness to let them into my heart.

Of course it's a very gradual process, but over the years the rigid discrimination I made between friends, enemies and strangers is gradually giving way to a feeling of trust.

Chapter 4

THE JOYFUL LAND

After the Chinese invaded Tibet in nineteen fifty-nine, many Tibetans escaped over treacherous mountain passes into India; among them some of the most senior lamas. Although they could carry with them few possessions, they carried in their hearts the wisdom gained from decades of study, debate and contemplation. Some of these lamas settled in Dharamsala, and when the hippy movement was at its height, lamas and hippies met and the cultural exchange began. Many young Tibetans were captivated by Western ideas and technology, but others already saw that Western materialism had not made us any happier but had instead brought us great problems. Why else would so many young people turn their backs on their comfortable lives in search of a spirituality they could not find within the constraints of their sophisticated society? Why would these Westerners choose to put up with the hot, overcrowded conditions in Dharmasala unless they were disillusioned with Western values? I was also disillusioned with my life and wanted to find a better way of living, but could not afford to travel, and was hampered by my poor sight. As more Westerners travelled to India and the reputation of the Tibetan Lamas spread, some hippies became students of the lamas, even learning Tibetan and translating texts into English.

After a while a few lamas were invited to the West to teach. Teaching courses were being established right here in England, specially designed for Westerners. Although the West was materially much richer than the

East, the lamas soon saw that Westerners had more mental problems. They knew that all suffering arose in the mind and could be removed through correct study and meditation. So While Western scientists developed medicine to manage the symptoms of mental diseases, the lamas had the medicine to eradicate the very root of mental sickness. This was not in bottles or tablets. It was spiritual advice, advice that had been tried and tested since the time of the Buddha.

One of these high lamas was His Holiness Kyabje Zong Rinpoche, who visited Manjushri Institute in England in the summer of nineteen eighty-one.

Zong Rinpoche was a tall, erect eighty year-old with a distinctive white beard and natural charm. For two weeks he taught tirelessly in the Meditation Hall at Manjushri to about one hundred eager students. When not teaching, he gave personal interviews to any individual student that requested them, as well as advice on ritual.

The course began after much preparation and excitement with prayers and meditation. Rinpoche then followed an ancient text, explaining the meaning of every paragraph and showing how we could apply it to our daily life to make our lives happy and meaningful.

The following week Kyabje Zong Rinpoche offered a Tantric empowerment to the students who were interested. The students came respectfully into the room and prostrated to the venerable Lama on the throne, then sat on cushions on the floor to still their minds with quiet breathing meditation or a few mantras.

Rinpoche, who had spent the day in preparation and meditation, now began to chant from the text. Few of us understood much of the Tibetan. After the chanting the translator explained the meaning in English, or told us what to visualise and what state of mind to generate.

We began by offering a mandala.

A mandala offering is a short ritual by means of which we offer the entire universe in a symbolic form, including everything that is dear to us and all living beings such as our family and friends, even our enemies and strangers. In this way everything should be visualised as completely pure and offered to the Buddhas, keeping nothing for ourselves.

After this the Bodhisattva vows are recited. This purifies our mind and reminds us that the purpose of the empowerment is to attain enlightenment as soon as possible so we will have the power to lead everyone to the same joyful state. From one point of view the path to enlightenment is a long and lonely path, from another point of view it is an exciting shared adventure.

I would love to share this wonderful experience with family and friends, but for the moment will have to travel alone. I would love to take everyone who has formed part of my life, including the Sisters of Mercy who tormented me when I was a school child. But spiritually I am still a child, powerless to help anyone.

Today I am being offered the chance to develop such power, by a lama who undoubtedly has it himself: 'Fearless like the King of the Lions, his radiance dispels the fears of all who behold him.' This description of Buddha Shakyamuni from Geshe Kelsang's book The Bodhisattva Vow, could well apply to Zong Rinpoche; he had such presence, such majesty. And at that moment, sitting at his feet, I was richer than the richest man, rich with a wealth that cannot be lost or stolen by others.

Everyone in this hot stuffy room is now my spiritual brother or sister; travelling companions on this spiritual journey up the mountainside to enlightenment, led by our incomparable Guide.

I have heard it said the further along the path you

progress, the fewer companions you have to share the journey with, but for now I was surrounded by spiritual friends.

I have to make this Bodhisattva promise or vow to the best of my ability, beginning in small ways to fulfil my promise to benefit others and not falter. When things get difficult, as they inevitably will from time to time, I can write to Zong Rinpoche and ask for his advice and blessings. Or I can pray to the Buddhas for guidance and protection.

Two years later, in the summer of nineteen eighty-three, His Holiness Kyabje Zong Rinpoche returned to Manjushri Centre again to teach 'The Hundreds of Deities of the Joyful Land.

This is like a Buddhist Heaven that we pray to take rebirth in so we can reunite with our spiritual teachers and continue on the path to enlightenment for the benefit of all suffering beings including ourselves.

As well as this he offered us more advice on our personal practice. I find it hard to comprehend my own good fortune at having attended these teachings and sat at the feet of such a great sage. And in the future I intend to visit this Joyful Land.

The following day was bright and sunny and as we sat on the wall opposite the main entrance to Conishead Priory, sipping our tea and enjoying the warm sun. My friend, who had no wish to take part in this week's programme, asked me, 'Empowerment - what power?'

I explained, 'The least I can expect to gain from this empowerment is that for some time afterwards I will experience a feeling that my mind is more peaceful and controlled and I will be happier than before. This happiness heals the mind but comes from the mind. I can't heal my mind with tablets, nor can I arrange my life in such a way that no problems occur, but if my mind is happy none of these problems will disturb me.

Is that not power? This is an immediate benefit of taking the empowerment. After that I hope to have the power to fulfil my promise; the power to lift my mind out of its familiar rut and put it on the road to full enlightenment. Having reached enlightenment I will have the skill to help everyone else with their problems and suffering, regardless of their own beliefs or faith. This is what I hope to obtain from the empowerment.'

Questions like this one are very welcome as they enable me to look at my own beliefs and experiences. In fact when Lama Yeshe gave the empowerment of Chittamani Tara in the summer of nineteen seventy-nine, I felt quite detached from the people who I had daily contact with. Giving this situation some thought I realised I myself had changed during that week, and this sense of being a stranger in a familiar place came not from my surroundings but from myself. I had become a new person, and it was this new person who was the stranger. Little by little, however, the new me started to become more familiar and less strange.

My mind jostles gently in cold winter wind
Thoughts batter about in my head in disarray,
Fear and pleasure, like nightmares in the day.
Cold winter wind numbs my brow,
Freezes thoughts in motion.
Now I see my mind like a calm sea,
A frozen lake.
Don't chip the ice but leave to thaw,
Gently; so gently let it move once more.

There was no doubt the empowerment had changed me for the better. All the unwashed bodies squashed into the hot and overfilled room those two weeks were my spiritual brothers and sisters. The bond was palpable and, as a man from New Zealand observed, apart from our collective interest in Buddhism we had little in common. Our common bond was this Lama and when he passed away on November 15th nineteen eighty-three, the world had lost a great teacher and a great sage. Language was no barrier to such a person and I could not feign wisdom sitting at his feet. He knew. He just knew.

The only limitation in his presence was my own lack of ability to comprehend the vastness of the wisdom and compassion he manifested to help us. How lonely his life must be when only he could truly comprehend its meaning. Surely he has taken rebirth in this world to benefit pitiful beings, and none more pitiful than myself. I pray I may have the good fortune to meet him again in another realm; somewhere, somehow, I must find him and sit again at his feet, feel the warmth of his laughter, and once more have my pride cut down with his sword of wisdom.

Finally, through his inspiration and guidance, I too will become like him: fearlessly I will shake the world and gather all beings into my heart, and carry them to freedom from fear and torment. Meanwhile I have to follow his shining example of effortless purity. After all, he has empowered me to follow him to the Joyful Land. Having bought the ticket, it is up to me to make this journey to liberation and the Buddhafields. But how?

The Lama now describes in detail the meditations which I must practice from now on if I am to succeed. He describes the colour; shape and attributes of a meditational Deity and the lotus throne that all the Buddhas sit or stand on. Then he offers the mantra and explains its power to assist. Mantra, he tells us, is protection for the mind. The Deity just described is a perfect faultless Buddha.

I have now been given the power to actually become

such a perfect Buddha in the same aspect. I can purify my speech and protect my mind with the mantra. I now have a Sadhana to practice, ritual prayers to recite daily. Depending on my past karma and the strength of my faith I will at some time in the future become this perfectly enlightened Buddha and be able to liberate all beings directly.

Now I know that the place to meditate is in my heart and as my interest in the external world decreases my inner world is enriched. When finally I give up this obsessive quest for my own, externally based happiness in this life, at the same time I will have freed myself from the problems of this life. I will have however a wealth of life experience to share with others and hope to be able to use all of this in the future.

At the end of the teachings we all offered a thanking mandala to Zong Rinpoche. Is there a greater kindness than to show how to overcome all of life's problems?

We then filed past him one by one and offered the traditional scarf to the Lama, who returned it by putting it around our neck as a blessing. Thanking him, we left the room tired but elated after so many hours of concentration.

In Tibet it was customary to offer these specially made white scarves as an expression of gratitude and respect. They were symbolic rather than practical, being more like cobwebs than cloth they would hardly have kept out the Tibetan cold. But at least they were an offering even poor Tibetans could afford. Although it is a beautiful practice, it is not part of our culture and in the Buddhist Centres I *visit* in the West it is no longer done. I *do* miss these touches of Tibetan culture which added magic and mystery to my early days of Western Buddhism, although I can accept that we are not Tibetans and don't need to import their culture, we do need their wisdom.

Having said this I cannot help missing the original Tibetan chanting and I can even envy those who came after the translations were completed as they have nothing to compare the English versions with. However over the years I have become familiar with the English tunes and I have to admit that I could not understand the Tibetan, any more than I could understand the Latin Mass. Although both have a timeless quality, it doesn't fit comfortably into the hectic pace of modern life.

Now that Buddhism has been translated into so many new languages the wisdom of the East is accessible to far more people, even if it upset some dinosaurs like myself.

Chapter 5

PEACE AND HAPPINESS

I made my way slowly out of the stuffy room through the chattering crowds and hurried along the cool, dim cloisters to the front door of the building. The sun was dazzlingly bright and it was a relief to feel the clean warm air on my face after concentrating for such a long time. Simon, a friend who was visiting for the week, had already reached the door and was waiting patiently for me.

At last we could enjoy the sunshine as we walked through the woods to the bay. The nettles were at their height and the canopy of tall leafy trees hummed with thousands of winged things; whatever they were they did not descend to eat us, which made walking relaxing. We had been sitting on our meditation cushions for what had seemed an eternity while a nun led a meditation on: 'Taking and Giving.'

As we walked along under the shady trees, I asked Simon, 'Is it possible that through this very simple meditation on 'Taking and giving' I can actually take on the suffering of others simply by imagining it dissolves into my heart; visualised as thick black smoke?'

How fantastic! Then when the smoke has completely disappeared, I must believe I have freed everyone from suffering. Now I imagine my heart transforms into a brilliant white crystal, which radiates light in all directions healing the bodies and minds of others, until the whole universe is filled with healing light.

What was even more exciting: if I become very

familiar with this through daily meditation I can combine it with my breathing. But even then without faith and self belief it will never work.'

Now I asked Simon, 'How is it possible to benefit everyone through this simple meditation?'

'Through the strength of our faith and imagination.'

Simon continued to speak in a thoughtful manner, 'When I can do this, then not one moment of my life will be wasted, but will bring peace and happiness to all.'

'But how long will it take for me to do this meditation effectively?'

'Right now this meditation will probably not have much effect other than pacifying your own mind for a short time; however in time and with regular practice it will become much more powerful and I have no doubt that anyone who does this meditation regularly will be able to remove the suffering of others in the future. How long it takes depends on the effort I put into my practice.'

'So it can be done either to relieve the suffering of just one person or a whole group of people?

For example, I could concentrate on my mother, if she was suffering from cancer? Or the problems of those caught up in a flood?'

'Yes, that's right.'

'But I feel that before I can help anyone else I should first begin by removing my own problems, surely that would make me a better meditator?

Now Simon quoted from a text by Geshe Chekawa (1102-1176) which said, "Begin the sequence by taking from your own side."

'According to my understanding that means exactly that.'

I thought about Simon's words as we picked our way slowly along the narrow, winding path that wound its way through the shade of the dense rhododendrons, and on towards the bay.

So first I need to begin with myself by overcoming my own mental suffering and problems, then I will have more power to help others.'

This advice was only a few words but could change me for the rest of time. Why had I not heard it before?

As we walked towards the bay, the path widened and tall trees gave way to the bright water and distant hills. Simon, who had also been brought up as a Catholic, said, 'Respecting the values of others is the foundation of peace and harmony, so at this time when everything is being compared and measured, would it not be refreshing to look at the similarities and disregard the differences?

With our meditation on taking and giving we can help everyone, not just Buddhists!

'In countries that traditionally practice the faith, the prisons are full of Buddhists; while in traditionally Christian countries, they are full of Christians, so how can we say that one religion is better than another? If someone refrains from killing, stealing, or any other wrong action, what does it matter what religion they profess?'

I had to agree.

In the interim between leaving Catholicism and finding Buddhism my simple rule had been to treat others as I would like to be treated myself, but it was not always easy.

Now I have been shown how to do this wonderful meditation which can actually help all beings, in time I will be able to help them all.

According to Buddhism unfairness is not possible because karma, the simple law of cause and effect acts like a pendulum and just as a pendulum swings steadily from side to side so the steady swing of cause and effect keeps a perfect balance between actions and their effects. When the pendulum swings towards a good action it has no choice but to swing back producing a good result and when it swings towards a bad action it will inevitably bring a bad result.

'With this meditation I can absorb the bad karma that is in the world and replace it with good karma, gradually filling the world with loving kindness. This is so simple it can be understood by everyone.'

As we walked through the bright sunlight we debated how to use this meditation to benefit others in our daily life. Simon said that all of us have done both good and bad actions in the past and now with this meditation on taking and giving we have the opportunity to accumulate much more merit, which will over time remove our own karmic debt. Eventually this investment in good karma will eliminate the results of our bad actions as well as the propensity to create more.

I did agree with Simon's statement in theory, but in practice it would not be so easy. Much of the suffering I had experienced during my childhood still had the power to hurt me.

There was no doubt that it still felt unfair. In fact if this was my only life then it was unfair.

But now, as a Buddhist, I had to admit to myself that I have created the cause for all my experiences in a past life. By admitting my own responsibility, I could then go on to forgive those who had caused me so much pain. Simon reminded me I should try to practice what I had been taught as a Catholic – to forgive and turn the other cheek. The rationale behind it may be different, but the practical, ethical response is the same.

I knew that Simon was right, but letting go completely would take time and effort. So I asked Simon, 'If I follow the moral discipline of a practising Buddhist, will I have more in common with a devout practising Catholic or Jew than with a Buddhist who ignores his vows?'

'Um, I take your point, but what really matters here is not so much what religion you profess but rather that it would never be right to pretend to yourself that you are better than you are. This would surely close the door to becoming better. Surely in Buddhism it is not necessary to be perfect at the beginning – as we know that we have many lives to improve before we become enlightened?'

'Several years ago I came across a wonderful quote, *"Whatever man can conceive, man can accomplish."* Think about it Simon! If I conceive myself as an essentially ordinary, limited and faulty being, this mind will prevent me from making this meditation a reality. An ordinary being could never have the power to remove the suffering from others simply by imagining absorbing it into his own heart and then sending out light rays with the power to heal the minds and bodies of others.'

Simon hesitated a while before answering me, 'As long as you believe you are incapable of helping others this way, this conception will prevent you from succeeding in this meditation or for that matter of becoming an enlightened being yourself, for this we need strong faith in our own ability to help others.'

By attending this course I have found the inspiration to develop faith in my own potential. And I now know I must believe strongly in my ability to transform my mind and not obstruct my own progress by clinging to the belief that I can't.

'Yes, Simon, I know that. I should just go for it. However the go for it mind does not arise easily.'

'You are talking about a very high level of self-respect. Do you think it is possible to be an honest and good person if you do not have a religion, as long as you have self-respect?'

'Definitely. Many of the kindest people I have met do not adhere to any faith. They are simply good people. But if I had never heard of the idea of enlightenment myself, I would not be able to conceive of it as a possibility, would I?'

At this point we reached the shore, the tide was in and the sky was cloudless; the hills on the other side of the bay were bathed in sunlight. In the distance on our left, beyond the railway viaduct stood the Old Man of Coniston, gracing the head of the bay. We sat down on some warm dry grass. Little yellow flowers carpeted the stony ground like little stars at our feet.

Sometimes Paula and I walked along the beach northwards from Manjushri Institute towards the mouth of Ulverston canal. When we got close to the long, low man-made hill by the Glaxo chemical factory, Paula became fearful. The pile of jagged rocks which formed a slag heap from the old iron works cast an eerie shadow over the pebbly beach on warm sunny days. It was so ugly and barren that Paula and I called it the moon. The only life on the 'moon' was stone crop, which grew all over the brittle and acrid smelling slag heap transforming it into a moon garden; each summer when it was covered with little yellow star-shaped flowers, Paula and I called them 'moon flowers', as they carpeted the stony surface.

Perhaps like this, my own dark heart could flower during my meditation and I could send out lights in all directions to bring peace and happiness to everyone they touched.

Some distance away two men were loading stones into buckets and taking them to their car. Why, I can't imagine.

'Sometimes it looks like people are grabbing little bits of universe and squashing them into their pockets for personal use,' Simon continued, 'Do they not realise that they are standing on a flood plain and it would be more appropriate to be adding stones to it rather than taking them away? If the planet is plundered continually in this way then the danger of floods and famine will increase. Although that is only a small action, if we all did it, very soon the foreshore would shrink alarmingly.'

I had to agree.

'Even in the short time that I have lived here the shoreline has eroded dramatically, due to high seas and winds. But Simon, by the same measure, surely if everyone did some small positive action every day then the collection of good deeds would soon amass and the results be felt by all?'

'Some people just don't think the time will come when this world is no longer habitable, but the way to other worlds is not through throwing expensive metal tubes into the air and looking for life on Mars.

'How many people alive now will live on the moon or Mars? There is so much emphasis on exploring other planets, but that money could be spent on relieving the poverty and suffering on our own planet.'

I had to admit that such thoughts rarely entered my very unscientific mind, but it made sense.

'The journey I need to make is free, it will harm no one; it will bring only happiness to me and to others. This journey is of course the Bodhisattva path to enlightenment, the journey of the mind from self interest to caring for others. I can begin this voyage right now, without the need for expensive technology, but it will take me further than any rocket NASA will launch. If I waste my life in meaningless actions such as trying to fly to the moon I will not reach the Buddha Lands but will be thrown into a miserable future created by my own deeds. In this way my Buddhist practice is creative.'

Sitting here with Simon I was reminded of the summer course that I had attended in the summer of nineteen seventy-nine. It was the first time I had met Lama Yeshe and Lama Zopa, who had come from India on their teaching tour for a couple of weeks. Arriving at the front door I had looked into the dark cavernous entrance to the cloisters.

It was almost seven o'clock and everyone was rushing into the chapel for morning meditation. But when I turned my back on the bright morning sun to go into the cool shady doorway, a loud and rebellious voice cried out from inside me, 'NO!' so I turned around and walked down to the bay through the woods filled with singing birds and the sweet smell of woodland flowers and the gentle rustle of trees, as the early morning bees buzzed by and flies hummed high in the branches. As no one was around to hear I sang loudly to myself:

May everyone be happy,
May everyone be free from suffering,
May no one ever be separated from their happiness,
May everyone have equanimity free from hatred and
attachment.

Of course Simon knew these words well as we chanted them often to generate the mind of Bodhichitta.

On reaching the shore I had wondered if I ought to feel guilty for turning my back on the morning meditation. But as the bay was deserted, there had been no one to answer my question so I had answered it myself, 'No, I don't need to feel guilty at all. I had listened to the needs of my inner voice.'

Looking over to the line of trees on the hilltop at the other side of the bay I had become aware of something blue on the ground. Someone had placed a small stone upright in the pebbles. Written on it were the words:

'The best things in life are free, but Buddhism doesn't come cheap.'

It was true that the course had to be paid for but this statement made me mad. First I thought to throw the stone away but then I decided to answer on a small stone tablet of my own. I found a similar sized stone, and digging in the bottom of my bag, found a blue crayon of Paula's, which I must have picked up while tidying the flat. I wrote:

'Samsaric life is cheap as shit
And I have had enough of it.'

I set my stone tablet next to the first one so that people could read them both.

I recounted this story to Simon and explained that at first I was angry then felt sad that these people had not understood the real meaning of the teaching from the Lamas. I saw how lucky I was, thanks to these people.

In fact I could not afford the course either but who could put a price on wisdom? When the time came to pay my bill I had to beg the director for a discount, which he kindly made.

Simon sat quietly looking at the distant hills as I rambled on. I enjoyed debating with Simon.

'As I was born into a Christian family, in a Christian country, I had no choice but to absorb this culture. But there had always been an underlying unease, a sense there must be more to life. Somehow this way was too simple, there was something missing.'

Simon agreed with me that his upbringing also felt as if it lacked something and that he had begun his quest for the truth with a Theravadan Buddhist monk many years before he found this tradition. His words took me back several years.

'Never did this feeling, that there is more to life, strike me more than when I was married and pushing Paula in her pram up Station Road towards Whitley Bay Station. The day was perfect, just like this one; warm and sunny with a clear, cloudless sky, and I was going back home to my husband in Otterburn Avenue in Monkseaton on the train, a married woman with a lovely house and a perfect baby.

'As I took Paula out of the pram, a woman stopped and commented that I must be blessed to have such a beautiful baby. I had to agree. But not so long ago my mother had also pushed a pram up this road, on her way back to a lovely house and husband. How soon would it be before Paula would be pushing her baby up Station Road in a pram? Was this really such a perfect day? And I wondered; was this the most life was able to offer, or was there a greater meaning that was eluding me?

'I could find no fault with my life at that time but somehow there was something missing. How could I find my real purpose? Animals also have homes partners and babies. Surely human life must have some purpose beyond the activities we share with animals?'

Simon said I had better stop here as we needed to hurry back up through the woods to sit at the feet of Lama Yeshe, who will explain to us the real meaning of life.

I was glad I had taken out a little time to walk on the beach with Simon, and we hurried back up through the woods and returned to the crowds refreshed. Sometimes things are just meant to be and listening to the inner voice is important.

We gulped down a cup of tea and ran up to the meditation room where Lama Yeshe was due to give a talk.

Lama Yeshe was here for two weeks and people had come from all over the world to listen. Many of the students had followed him from India and would continue to follow him when he left on his annual teaching tour, calling in wherever he was invited to teach before finally returning home to India. Lama Zopa had also come with him and their teachings were staggered so that it was possible to attend talks from both Lamas.

At last Lama Yeshe entered the room, only twenty minutes late. The chant master had suggested that we chant mantras together until he arrived.

`OM MUNI MUNI MAHA MUNIYE SOHA-
OM MUNI MUNI MAHA MUNIYE SOHA... `

The sound echoed throughout the room, flowing down the stairs and out through the open windows, filling all of space, even permeating my flesh and raising goose pimples all over my body. I loved this Buddha Shakyamuni mantra; so few words, but so much power. I hoped that Buddha's timeless wisdom was filling my mind right now.

I sat up and tried to listen attentively. Listening to Lama Yeshe is actually not very difficult as he has a way of making everything sound interesting while at the same time getting over his point. Today he began by explaining that our main problem was dissatisfaction, that we spent so much time seeking satisfaction but never finding it: even borrowing a few words from Mick Jagger to make his point. The time flew by, and when the teaching was over I went with the crowd to eat lunch. But rather than seeking satisfaction, I tried to feel content with what was actually on my plate.

Chapter 6

SO MUCH LOVE

I was still very new to Buddhism and the intensity of the course was challenging, with so many people milling around in a relatively small space. My reading vision at this time was perfect; I could read the smallest print without glasses and my distance vision was good enough to count the trees on the horizon. However my field of vision was severely restricted and when I moved about I could only see a small area directly in front of me. There was little point in protesting that I had eyesight problems, as I had made the mistake of doing while debating with someone. After finding out I could see things both close up and far away, my neighbour insisted my eyesight was perfect and the problem was all in my head.

In fact, although I was at this time registered partially sighted; even I did not know exactly what this meant for other partially sighted people as everyone's eyesight is unique. What could another partially sighted person see? All I can say is that my own sight varied from day to day according to light and dark conditions and that, in general, I could expect my sight to get worse over the next few years until finally I could see nothing at all.

Often kind people stop to chat. They are curious to explore my grey world, a world that in the future will be devoid of any shape or colour except those I have pieced together by my imagination, based on memory and tactile sensations, as well as smells, tastes and sounds, but for the moment I still had my very limited field of vision. It was rather like living life through a keyhole.

It can be a dull world and surely the least interesting subject for a blind person like me to focus on. It never seems to occur to people how interested I would be in their brightly coloured lives; filled with subtle gestures and expressions that I no longer have the opportunity to see.

Possibly they do not speak of these things to me out of consideration, but the truth is that news from the sighted world is the most exciting topic there is for a blind person enshrouded in the dark mist of their disability. Sighted people take the world of shapes and colours as their birthright, as I too once did, but now I would cherish any vicarious glimpses of that world I could catch if people would only describe its wonders to me from time to time. I sometimes wonder why people find my drab and shapeless world so fascinating.

They also say how brave I am, which is something else I don't understand. I am no braver than anyone else, just more limited. At that time I still had not summoned up the courage to ask a Lama what I had done in a previous life to lose my sight in this one. But a couple of years later I had an interview with a visiting Lama and he found my fear of the truth quite amusing. When he had finished laughing at my plight in a kindly sort of way, he said that it was not a big problem and that I would probably overcome it in the next two or three lives. This may sound a heartless reaction, but when asking a Lama for advice it is essential to be prepared for an unexpected, or even an unwelcome reply.

Strangely, the answer made me see that it really was not a big problem; the bigger problem was to focus on my future lives rather than wasting time and energy on something that could not be resolved in this life. Then he advised me to help others with similar problems.

Although I could now see that from the perspective of countless past and future lives my defective eyesight is quite unimportant, on a day-to-day level it still made life quite difficult. A normally sighted person cannot possibly understand how impaired vision affects an individual. When someone breaks a leg it is not so difficult for others to see the problem, but defective eyes are not in plaster and to the onlooker they can look perfect.

The following afternoon there were three hundred pairs of shoes left outside the chapel where Lama Zopa was about to give a talk, and I searched around for a space to put my own, so that I could find them when I came out a couple of hours later.

Three hundred people inside the chapel was rather too many for comfort and I was sitting in the centre of the chapel in a sea of sweaty humanity. It was past lunch time and I was hot, tired and hungry as Lama Zopa analysed the nature of phenomena.

Lama Zopa was explaining that we think the world consists of discreet things, separated from each other and from our minds which are perceiving them. We feel that things are 'out there,' solid, real and attainable. But when we search for things analytically, in the way that Lama Zopa was doing right then, they disappear into a seamless web of inter-relationships. There is nothing out there we can catch hold of, such as rainbows or the dancing shapes of light in a moving pool; they appear clearly but we can't catch hold of them.

As I was listening, suddenly I had the impression that Manjushri's sword of wisdom reached out from a painting hanging in the front of the meditation room and sliced up my body. The pieces of meat lay in a bloody wet pile on the carpet. Then the sword cut up the person on my right, then the person on my left, until there were no people left in the room, just a mixed up mass of flesh, blood and bones. It was no longer possible to distinguish one person from another. There were no friends, enemies or even strangers, just a homogenous mass of humanity.

This experience was somewhere between a daydream and a vision, but its impact was profound.

Although for me the lesson came in a very dramatic, gruesome visual form, we can arrive at the same conclusion in a gentler way. Just ask yourself, 'Where do I end and where does the world begin?' When we breathe in, exactly at what point does the air become part of our body? Or when we eat or drink, when does the food and water stop being part of the outside world and start being part of us? Or, on a subtler level, when you read these words, when do the ideas they express stop being someone else's and become yours? Thinking about it, it is obvious that there is no clear boundary; we make the boundary where we choose to. It's the same with everything.

If we could see the cycles of water, minerals, and the energy of sunlight, would it still be so obvious to us where the limits of a tree are?

The more you think about it, the more you see that everything depends on everything else, and the only reason we see a world made of discreet things and people is that our thoughts have divided the world up in this way. In reality we cannot separate anything out from everything else – the separations we see are just those made by our thoughts.

This experience with Manjushri's sword taught me something else too. It was shocking to see my body chopped up. All my life I have cherished and cared for this body. If people insulted it I would become incensed. If it was wounded only slightly I would find it unbearable. I was so familiar with it I could hardly think of myself apart from it. But here I was, disembodied, looking at a pile of meat on the carpet. This body was not always my body, and there will come a time when it will cease to be mine. What is the sense of cherishing it so much, in such an exaggerated way? It is not really different from anyone else's. If someone else's body is hurt, does this matter less than if it is mine that is hurt? Surely all bodies are equally important? It certainly makes no sense to identify with this one body.

Until now my life has revolved around my body. I don't mean that I think about it all the time, trying to make it beautiful, comfortable, feeding it, cleaning it etc – although this does take up a great deal of my time, as it does most people's. What I mean is, that when I think of myself, I think of myself in a body, specifically as a woman of a certain age. And it is this embodied 'I' that is the centre of my universe. Nearly all my thoughts revolve around this 'I'.

I am completely obsessed. If I was so obsessed with anyone or anything else they'd consider me insane and lock me up. But being so obsessed with myself is considered normal. Now here I was, looking down at this chopped up mess on the floor and wondering how on earth this could be so important?

If instead of focusing so much attention on one body and one embodied person, why not cherish all bodies and all beings equally? As soon as I can step out, even momentarily, from the extreme self-obsession that I am normally trapped in, it is obvious that other people are far more important than me for the simple reason that there are lots of them and only one of me. What would happen if instead of being so wrapped up in myself I cherished only others, regarding their happiness, freedom, success and so forth as more important than my own?

The first thing that would happen is that my own problems would completely disappear. If the law of karma is true, then all my misfortunes are the result of my own dark actions and the basic reason I act in a negative way is because I feel that I am more important than others. So if I begin to consider others as more important than myself I would naturally stop committing negative actions and only engage in positive actions.

Also, when something unpleasant happens to me, it is my self-concern that makes this into a problem. When I look at my life from a self-centred point of view, I tend to forget that many people are suffering more and have much greater problems than me. But when I look at my life from a wider perspective I feel I am incredibly fortunate. Compared to the vast majority of people I am so rich, so fortunate to have discovered the Lamas who can teach me the real meaning of life and how to attain it. I was even lucky to have had an unhappy childhood, an unhappy marriage and most of the time to have lived in relative poverty. I sometimes ask myself, 'Should I thank the Sisters of Mercy for my present good fortune?' If I were rich and seduced by the promise of human friendship and security, would I have sought to renounce such fortune for a more austere lifestyle?

The sound of Lama Zopa's voice echoed in the great hall as he chanted the concluding prayers of dedication. Then we got up off our cushions and filed out past the throne. I clambered over the maze of cushions that were strewn over the cluttered floor and left the chapel while Lama Zopa continued to chant. The sound of the Tibetan chant, as wonderful as it was incomprehensible, faded as we left him sitting alone on the throne beneath the shrine.

Amazingly my shoes were where I left them, still next to the pillar. I would not have found them otherwise, lost among three hundred pairs. I put them on and went through the large front door and out into the sunlight. But the fresh air did not blow away the memory of the meat on the carpet. I didn't mention the experience of the wisdom sword to anyone as they might have thought I was mad, but I remained shaken from my firm belief that I was important. I can perhaps call this experience spiritual surgery. Something had been healed at a deep level.

In those early days no one was allowed to camp, so everyone squeezed into overcrowded dormitories with military metal bunk beds and straw and horse hair mattresses. Perhaps, after India, this was luxury, but for those with less experience of the hippy trail it must have been difficult and there were often tears and tantrums.

The crowds were very tiring and I sought quiet corners to sit in during the breaks. But I was lucky as my flat was just down the road and in the evenings Paula and I could leave the crowds and go home to sleep in our own comfortable beds.

The ten days melted away and the Lamas left for the next leg of their tour. People returned home to their jobs and the Priory became a sombre space for the rest of the summer. But when the autumn term began again in September, the mood would lift and Geshe Kelsang would begin to teach throughout the autumn until his Christmas course, teachings that would later become his books.

Alan, a friend, called at my flat and asked me to come to lunch at the Priory. After several protests, I reluctantly got up and we walked up the path in the wonderful hot sun and had lunch. Not wishing to return straight away I stayed and chatted to a couple of friends and the Tibetan translators on the grass by the main door. The conversation was light, and Tenzin, one of the translators, asked me if I could sit in full lotus? Samten, the other Tibetan monk, had got involved in a conversation with some casual visitors from Barrow. I explained I could sit in full lotus for an hour. Realising that this sounded a proud statement, I decided to purify right there by sitting on the ground for the next hour, in full lotus without moving from the spot. Meanwhile, the lady from Barrow continued with her questions, while her husband found a Western monk to debate with. The two Tibetans were capable translators but had little understanding of our western way of thinking, so finally Tenzin told her I would be better able to answer her questions, and sent her to me. She sat down on the wall in front of me, and explained that they were

Pentecostalist and her church would disapprove if they knew she had visited here. She then told me she regularly went up into her bedroom alone and sat on the chair to meditate, so she was very interested in our meditations. It seemed to me these people were on a secret visit to a forbidden land. Just as my brother David and I had loved the excitement of sneaking into our neighbour's gardens when we were young children to steal peas and rhubarb, this couple in their late seventies were still enjoying sneaking into the grounds of Conishead Priory to talk to Buddhist practitioners. I wondered whether they might like to have the excitement of sneaking back again to listen to our Tibetan teacher but she said they would not be able to return. It is not often I meet someone so open minded, and found her such an inspiration. Her interest in Buddhism had begun when their son had returned from travelling in India with many Buddhist books.

As she sat on the wall, her long blue coat a little out of place on such a warm summer day, she said sadly they would not be able to return, even though they only lived twelve miles away as neither of them were in good health and they did not dare antagonise the Pentecostal Church.

While she waited for her husband, we sat and talked. Looking across at the front door of the building, she now told me she had been blind as a child, not from birth but as the result of an operation that went wrong. But later she had miraculously regained her sight. Abruptly she stopped talking about her blindness, saying she did not know why she had mentioned it. Perhaps I did know why, but since the whole time I had been sitting in full lotus at her feet she could never have guessed the reason. After that she entered a little trance and quoted something about Joseph from the Bible, something I had not been taught as a child.   Her beautiful little trance ended with her saying over and over that I should never forget there is so much love in the world.

Chapter 7

MORNING LIGHT

A few years earlier I had been told of a place in Cumbria called *Morning Light* by a friend. Finding this address again and noticing that I lived nearby, I was intrigued and without further thought telephoned and asked for some information. I am not sure if they understood my question, but as the lady on the phone booked me in for a week I was soon to find out. I now know that *Morning Light* is a Christian sanctuary located on the shores of the deepest lake in England.

Wastwater is not like the other lakes, with their gondolas, yachts and crowds of tourists. The water is dark, deep and held in by a sinister backcloth of scree, which descends from the moody mountain on the opposite side of the lake and continues below the surface of the water to unknown depths. A silent, looming landscape, its oppressive grandeur relieved only by a large rocky islet crammed with squabbling terns, their white undersides flashing as they lifted their dark wings.

I had no idea what to expect of *Morning Light* – a beautiful name in an impressive location. This was certain to be an adventure.

Clive came to the door and invited me to join the other visitors in the lounge for a cup of tea. While waiting for tea I chatted to a lady who had visited before. She told me that Clive was a regression therapist but had previously been a car salesman. Looking at the furnishings I concluded he must have been a very successful car salesman.

The following morning after a vegetarian breakfast in the communal dining room, Clive invited me to discuss what kind of therapy I was interested in. He suggested I had some contact healing from Peggy, his wife, followed by regression therapy with him. I explained the problem of my encroaching blindness and we agreed a few regressions might give us some clues about the origin of the problem, and perhaps even indicate a solution.

Peggy, a quiet retired nurse, invited me into her private sitting room for a healing session before lunch. Compared to the sumptuous lounge this room was homely, with a warm fire in the hearth.

She got to work on my aura, moving quietly about as she healed me. She was not young, probably about seventy, and wore a soft blue sweater with a floral skirt. I suspect her own health could have done with a lift. Clive would have made a wonderful Baptist minister, but although they were obviously Christian, I deduced from the grace before meals that their brand of Christianity was a little less orthodox than that of a minister. He was a solid man who would have fitted comfortably into any conventional setting, and I struggled to place him as an alternative therapist. Where had his interest in healing come from and why had they come to this wonderful detached country house that had previously been occupied by the local minister? The following day Clive found a quiet space for my regression.

'When I count to five … What do you see?'

'I see a frog.'

'A frog?'

'Yes.'

'Look again. Now what can you see?'

'I see a young lady standing by a lake. She is dressed in a long pale green satin dress with a purple sash that falls softly from the waist. She has shiny black hair elaborately arranged on top of her head with a hair ornament.'

'What is she doing?'

'She is standing amongst exotic shrubs that fill the air with delicate perfumes of every kind. A willow weeps over the silent lake, its leaves fluttering gently in the soft morning sunlight. There is no one about. She is throwing food into the still water for the swans, their beady black eyes darting across the water; scanning for morsels of food among the lotus blossoms and craning their long white necks in a graceful arch, which is reflected on the surface of the clear water.'

'What kind of place is this?'

'It is a very quiet place, with no one about besides this lady.'

'Now think of yourself as this lady. What is your name?'

'Yukio.'

'And where do you live?'

'I live in a small white house near the water.'

'Go inside the house now. Are you in the house?'

'Yes.'

'What is it like, are there other people there?'

'No there is no one here, I live alone. But I think my servants are nearby.'

'Your servants?' said Clive in amazement, perhaps he was wondering why I claimed to live alone when two other people occupied my house.

'Yes I have two servants.'

'And what do you do? I found this question very strange, why did Clive think that I had to do anything?'

'I am very beautiful and artistic; I write poetry, paint and play a lute.'

'Are you a musician?'

'No, I am very talented, but I play the lute only for my owner, the lord of this area.'

'The lord? Why do you do that?'

'I play for him when he comes to see me.'

'But more than that, it was as if my whole life was a work of art; the art of being a woman, and the art of pleasure. The recipient of this pleasure was my benefactor, the Emperor. As long as I pleased him he would feed and clothe me.'

'Go forward to the time that you see him.'

Yukio spoke in a quiet shy voice, 'I am standing behind a large white pillar and peeping round it through a doorway. The door is open.'

'Why do you do that?'

'This is the temple. It is a very beautiful building with a golden roof. It is made of wood with three layers, one on top of the other, each layer smaller than the one below it. It must be a Japanese temple. The golden corners of the roof turn up towards the sky in graceful curves. My lord may be here today and I want to see him, but I am shy and just peep round the pillar to see if he has come.'

'Tell me about that, why are you there?'

'No special reason. I am shy and women are banned from going into the temple, I just want to attract his attention.'

'Tell me about the time he comes out.'

'We walk to where the swans are. It is very sunny.'

'What happens on this day? Tell me about it. Are you his wife?'

'No, I am not his wife. I am not a royal person.'

'Does he have a wife?'

'Yes.'

'Why does he come to you?'

'It is my duty to please him and a great honour.'

'Do you love him?'

'I don't understand. What is love? This is duty. When I was a very young girl my parents gave me to this very powerful Emperor as a gift. Now it is my duty to obey my parents by serving him. In this way I honour my ancestors.'

'Do you remember your parents?'

'No.'

'Do you never see them?'

'No. Honour is very important in my country.'

'Yukio, do you have any spiritual beliefs?'

'I am not sure. Not a sense of religion, but perhaps a sense of honour. I am proud to serve him like this.'

'You commune with nature a lot, don't you?'

'Yes.'

'And when he is in the temple celebrating his religious rituals you are not permitted to go in with him and have to wait outside.'

'Yes.'

'Would no woman be permitted in there, not even the Empress?'

'No, she never accompanies him.'

'Does he come to the temple regularly to celebrate his religious ritual?'

'I think, when he goes there, it is to support the monks by taking food and they eat together. He eats with the priests who live there and they give him instruction.'

'I see, and is it on these occasions that he meets with you?'

'Yes, but he comes to my house on many other occasions too.

I can see him entering my house now. '

'What is he wearing?'

'He is wearing bright blue elaborately embroidered clothes made of silk.'

'Did anyone come with him?'

'No, but I think a soldier is nearby guarding him and looking after his horse.'

'And what do you do?'

'I play the lute to please him. Miyomi, my servant, comes with two delicate cups of sweet smelling tea which we drink before going out into the garden to walk through scented carpets of flowers and watch the birds flitting in and out of the trees.'

'… and did you lie with this man?'

'Yes, it is a very great honour because he's a very important person. He is maybe an Emperor.'

'Are you not sure?'

'I do not know' but realising that Clive did not understand the culture of this past life regression either,

I answered him. 'I am not ashamed of it.'

'There is no reason why you should be, but does he have - I know that this may be a painful question - does he have more than one mistress?'

'Probably. But they are not here. What he does when he is not with me is of no interest to me, it is not my business. According to the customs of this country the lord has absolute authority and no one, neither I nor his wife would question this. So, for as long as he chooses to feed, clothe and house me I have some status. He is kind to me. He gives me gifts, sometimes maybe money. I am not poor. But I can never appear in public with him; that is his wife's role.'

'Have you borne him any children?'

'No.'

'When he lies with you is he gentle and tender?'

'Yes.'

'And where do you go to be together?'

'In wild places where there are no people, not in buildings.'

'In the forest or in trees?'

'In trees, no. I am not a monkey!'

'Um, and you are completely alone. Are there no body guards?'

'There may be, but they are some distance away. They do not dare to watch their lord, they would lose their lives.'

'So when he loves you it is out in the open and among nature?'

'Yes.'

'And is that a very beautiful experience?'

'Yes, he is very kind.'

'And you give yourself willingly to him?'

'Yes.'

'Was he there when you were feeding the swans near to where your dwelling is?'

'I don't know, perhaps he was.'

'You seem to be a very powerful draw for him. He must want you and love you very much. Do you think he loves you? It is very difficult to tell with people of your race - you talk about honour, loyalty and duty, and of course those things are important, but I don't know whether those are other words for what I would call love. What is your interpretation of this?'

'I do not understand what you mean by love. It is my duty to please him. He is happy with me and comes to me when he wants to relax. I am like a refuge for him.'

'You are like a sanctuary for him, a sanctuary of beauty and tenderness. Are you happy to live like this? I suspect you have been living like this for a number of years, since you were about sixteen or seventeen.'

'No, I was much younger than that. I am only eighteen now.'

'And you have never wished to marry?'

I found this question very strange, did Clive not realise that I was not free to choose a husband, I was the property of the Emperor.

'No, I am here to please this lord, not myself. It is my duty and an honour. I don't know what you mean by love. My pleasure comes from pleasing him alone.'

'And do you always have to meet him in secret?'

'We don't meet in secret; we meet in private. An Emperor has no need for secrets; he is *the* rule maker. But there are very strict rules that *I* have to live by.'

Clive continued to ask me about love. But I, Yukio, was from a different time and culture. What was important to Clive had no meaning for me. I explained again:

'I have no wish to marry.'

'Because of him?'

'Yes. He is a very important person.'

102

'But that's not why you love him is it, you love him for himself. Is not that so? Or do you have a great loyalty and respect for him?'

'It's loyalty. It is as if I help him to run the country by allowing him to come and be my friend. It is said the mistress of an important man can sometimes influence the way he conducts his life, even more than his wife. Because when he is with his mistress he has no other pressure on him. He can just be himself.'

'Do you go for walks with him?'

'Yes.'

'Where do you walk to?'

'We go where the swans were. It's very sunny.'

'What happens on this day?'

'He is taking his boots off ... and sits down on the grass. We are not talking. I am facing away from him, and lying on the ground.'

'Is there a reason why you are doing that?'

'No, but I am shy. He is the lord of this area; I cannot watch him in this very private moment. There does not seem to be any other reason.

'And does he make love to you again today?'

'Yes.'

He has bent down very close to me and turned my face towards him tenderly in his hands. I can feel the warmth of his breath as his lips move closer and for a moment all the beauty of our surroundings is forgotten and we are absorbed in our union.

'It seems to me, Yukio, that these are the moments that you live for. It seems to me that your whole life is dedicated to loving, serving and pleasing him. That's a word that we have not used yet. But I am just beginning to realise it is a very important word. It is very important for you to please your lord. Isn't it?'

'Yes.'

'And I feel that when I asked you about your

religion, I feel that perhaps your religion is pleasing your lord.'

'It is my duty to serve him, not to love him as he is the Emperor. And he owns all his subjects, including me.'

'Now I understand a little more about why you must pleasure him in every way you can - with your body, with your friendship, with your sweetness, with your quietness when he wishes to be quiet. If he does not want to talk then you are silent; if he wants to walk you walk with him; if he wants to relax or to laugh a little you know how to laugh with him. Now I think I understand what your life is like, where and how you live, and the devotion you have for this important man, you study him; you study his needs, his moods, his wants, and his wishes. And with devotion you pleasure him and please him that is the purpose and function of your life.

'Am I exaggerating?'

'No.'

'Tell me, Yukio, what happens to you? Go ahead a little now. Is everything still the same?'

'I can see his palace on the hill made of white stone or marble. It is like a fortress. But I can't go there because I am not a member of the court. Nothing will alter that. The Empress is from a very wealthy royal family, but that has brought her no happiness.'

Clive obviously did not understand the rigid protocol of this country. I had my role and his wife had hers. My function in life was to serve my lord and this was my reason for living. Not out of love, which for me was a shallow sentiment, but out of honour; honouring my own family whom I hardly remembered, and my ancestors.

'Is it usual for the lord to have a mistress?'

'I think it must be the custom.'

What Clive did not realise was that I had never even spoken to another man, I lived alone with my servants and rarely did I even meet another woman. Only those who instructed me in the arts.

'But I take it that if his wife had a lover that would be something else. That would not be allowed. Neither of course must you entertain another man. Even if you wanted to – which, I feel, you don't at all.'

'No, I am happy.'

'How long do you feel that his wife has been aware of your presence and your role?'

'Since I was given to this lord as a gift by my parents many years ago. As a woman she can't do anything about it. She does not have any power and has to accept it even if she does not like it.'

'Go along then a little further, Yukio. Go to a time when there is an important change for you. How old do you feel now?'

'Forty-five.'

'And is all well with you? Is your health still good?'

'Yes, but I think my lord is not healthy.'

'What do you feel is wrong with him?'

'Perhaps he can't come out of the palace anymore.'

'Is he paralysed?'

'I'm not sure. But I never see him again.'

'You still have not any children by him?'

'No.'

'Is it by design that you have never conceived a child by him?'

'Yes. It is one of the many rules that I live by.'

'How do you prevent conception?'

'I use a herbal birth control.'

'I see; something you have learned?'

'Yes.'

'Would it be correct to call you a geisha?'

'No, because geishas entertain many men.'

'Yes, and you just entertain one. You live to serve him and him alone.'

'Yes. There are very strict rules I have to live by.'

'So, you are forty-five now, and you are not able to see him because he has not been well. Go ahead just a little more now and tell me what happens. How do you adjust to this new situation?'

'He is very overweight. I think he is not healthy.'

'Do you feel this is some kind of disease?'

'Something like that.'

'What happens Yukio? Tell me about it please.'

'I don't hear any news of him again.'

'Can you accept that?'

'No.'

'So what are you going to do, are you going to try and see him?'

Tears rolled down my cheeks silently, 'I can't see him. That's part of the rules that I have to live by. I accept that I can't go.'

The idea of bending the rules to see him was unthinkable to me, as were so many of Clive's ideas throughout this regression. This life belonged to a different time and culture, and there were many aspects of it that I, Philippa, could not understand either. Yet I could see some of Yukio's values colouring my present life. No wonder I fit uncomfortably into modern society where such outdated ideas have no place.

After I left school it had not occurred to me that an adult could behave in any way other than according to the pure Christian values taught in school and at home, and it came as a great shock to me to find that most people had different values. I had been taught how to be a young lady and a good Catholic. How could I be prepared for the church choir master to allow his hands to roam freely over my fourteen-year old breasts in the presence of my parents; how could I know my college friend, Barry was more interested in sex than in me, or that a complete stranger could rape me when from my side the idea was incomprehensible?

After leaving school in my early teens, my understanding of love and marriage was gleaned more from reading *Snow White* than *The News of the World*. So I had some vague and idealistic idea of love and marriage, but the idea of raping strangers was to my mind incomprehensible. Just like Yukio, I felt I belonged to a different time and culture, where honesty and respect took precedence over self gratification and deceit. If Yukio had been educated alongside me she would have been taught how to be a young lady, and like me, would have acquired no skills to survive in the world as a single mother without paid employment as I had to. But unlike me she was the property of the rich local lord of that area and had been taught all the skills she needed to please him. Yet like me she did not have the skills to live among the poor villagers and beg for food, just as I was completely unprepared when my protected life as a Catholic schoolgirl ended and some years later I found myself as a single parent on the fringes of society. Neither of us was prepared for the poverty and hardship of our later lives. My own education was no more relevant than that of Yukio in preparing me for life in the outside world.

Even within St Anne's Girls High School I was no match for the difficult girls.

I can see how Yukio would have found my life difficult and I can also imagine I could have been happy in the quietly ordered life of perfection and beauty that was hers.

Then Clive asked, 'If you tried to alter or bend the rules to see him would you feel you were betraying him?'

'Yes, and myself, too.'

'So what can you do, Yukio?'

'Maybe drown in the lake.'

'Sorry?'

'Maybe drown in the lake. I am not sure what I can do, but I have no future.'

Clive sat upright, this idea was shocking.

'I want you to look at this very carefully now. Is that what you feel an inclination to do?'

'Yes. I have no choice and I feel a great sense of fear. There is no life for me now.

'Do you walk around for a long time with the weight of this wrapped around you like a great mantle of sadness?'

'Yes, I am nobody now. I have no money.'

'You feel that your life is finished?'

'Yes.'

'How long is it since you saw him?'

'Months.'

'Go ahead a little further and tell me what happens.'

'It is cold and damp now. My servants have left me and I have to leave my house.'

'You have become virtually a beggar.'

'Yes, but worse than that I am a beggar in silks and satins. It is obvious from my appearance I have been very rich and the poor villagers have no time for a rich beggar. As I wander alone and penniless, through hostile village streets, without the protection of my lord, I have no status. But I still have my honour. I left the area and although I could have begged for food, this sense of honour kept me from doing so.'

'This is very sad, very sad. How long did this degrading business go on?'

'The rest of my life.'

'The rest of your life?' And how long is the rest of your life?'

'It's not long.'

'You decided not to end your life in the lake then?'

'I just starved to death.'

'You literally starved to death?'

'Yes.'

'I see. How very sad. Will you now go on to the day when you experienced the death of this physical body? Where are you when you die?'

'I just went into the woods and faded away through cold and hunger. I am too weak to walk any further. I lie down on a carpet of dead leaves that cover the frosty ground and my eyes close.'

I (Philippa) looked at my old body lying on the ground, pale and lifeless in the winter woodland. It is late afternoon and a chill white moon has already risen in the winter sky. As I watched, a white thread, like a plume of smoke rose into the air. This was my consciousness leaving that body and going to the next life.

I explained to Clive that I was safe, free from fear of wild animals, and from hunger, cold and heat. Normally I was afraid of great heights. But now I felt fearless as I floated above the frosty woodland, bodiless like a cloud. My interest in that life had dissolved into vapour, gone for good.

'Do you feel any fear at leaving your physical body?'

'No. I feel very peaceful.'

'Do you go and observe your love, because you could go there now, couldn't you?'

Although I had lost all interest in this life, Clive obviously hadn't.

'Do you do that? Do you go into the shining places of your own soul?'

'I don't think I go to see him.'

I had no wish to go. Clive could not understand my lack of interest and felt that saying goodbye to my lord was the most important part of the healing process.

In contrast, I, as a Buddhist, felt that grasping at that life which had already ended would obstruct my progress towards enlightenment. I had completely lost interest in Yukio's life and needed to move on to my next life, so there was no value in looking back. For me the fact I had lost interest was more relevant. But right now I was aware this conflicted with Clive's philosophy and for the duration of this regression I was willing to accept these now unfamiliar ideas as a healing tool.

Throughout the regression part of my mind was aware of my identity as Philippa, but it was Yukio herself who did not wish to return to see her lord. Although she had lived her whole life in his service, she did not understand the meaning of the word love. For her the nearest thing was duty and honour - the opposite of self-gratification. She had done her duty, and now she was free.

'You just closed your eyes in the woods and went into the long sleep of death?'

'Yes.'

'And when you woke up, Yukio where did you find yourself?'

After a very long pause, Clive asked, 'Do I correctly suspect that a part of you has never woken up? Never opened her eyes and found herself alive and well? Tell me, Yukio, as you are lighter, warmer, brighter and more and more peaceful, can you see well now? And where should you go?'

'I can see the tops of houses. And water on the right; it's like being in a balloon floating south over Lancashire. The grey slate tiles are wet with rain.'

'I want you now to make the link with the light of your higher consciousness, and feel the peace, beauty and light shining into Yukio's eyes when she finally opens those very sad eyes that had gone into a long and very unhappy sleep. She opens those eyes and she sees the light is entering. She is very happy and peaceful knowing that her true love will always be found in the shining realms; for in truth there is never any separation at all anyway. We are just playing many different roles that come together in the garden of our greater self.

'Before you come back I want to finally remind you that you stood for a long while in that party in Newcastle, the night when Barry told you that he was leaving you. And I believe that for a long time after that you were as much Yukio as you were Philippa. When you said you were a long way away you were with her, and she was with you. Your senses, particularly your sense of sight had in fact gone to sleep. You closed your eyes and just went into a long decline of sadness and depletion, as she did at the end of her life. But whenever you look at that party in your mind there is a Japanese girl standing there, feeling lost and helpless, as if her world had come to an end.

'There is no more important thing in life than to love and be loved. Without this there is nothing to live for. The one person that you lived for and loved, the only person that you really cared for or had been able to love, except for Teddy, was suddenly no more. He was withdrawn from your physical reality and your awareness. If you super-impose over yourself at that time the image of Yukio, with her feelings of unbearable sadness, hopelessness and abandonment, then you will understand what you, Philippa, went through at that party. And remember Yukio went into a long sleep long before she had closed those eyes under the trees, because her heart went to sleep when she could no longer see her lord.

'Feel the energy of Yukio's unhappiness and sublime sense of love gradually dissolving and being released from its physical overlay. As it does so, it ceases to interfere with your present body and brain and nervous system and thereby impair your senses. I am not suggesting for one moment that that is the only chapter of your soul that we need to look at to open your vision. But it is an important one. A very important one, because I think it reveals a deep reason for the way your whole life changed at that party. A big part of you died then and there was a withdrawal of something. Was it the same withdrawal as Yukio's?

'Was the feeling that overwhelmed her the same as that which overwhelmed you that night - and in a way forever since? I feel there is much here to understand. And when you understand yourself, then you can truly love yourself.'

'Do you still feel like Yukio?'

'No I have forgotten about her.'

'But you look at peace. Is Yukio at peace?'

'Yes.'

'Do you think that she will find her true love there in the shining world?'

'I think she is very happy.'

'I'm glad. I am also very glad that she has come from the long, long sleep and opened her eyes and she can see really well.

'Thank the shining lady of your higher self for this time of revelation, understanding and illumination. Know that this illumination will affect the etheric envelope around the physical body. In this envelope there are all the faces and impressions of all the many lives of the soul; and we know Yukio's face now is peaceful, and her eyes are open.

'From life to death to the bright and beautiful life of the shining world; thank you for the help and love and kindness that you have given us.

'I ask now for Philippa, that she slowly and

peacefully returns to her normal consciousness. Very gently, just as Yukio would walk down to see the swans, in her stillness and solitude. There is so much of her in you. Come back quietly now as I count from five down to one; when I get to number one when you are ready open your eyes. Feel that you have brought the sun of Yukio back into your awareness. When you have come back through the senses hold her; understand her in the mind of your heart. Five, four, three, two, and at one your awareness has come back to a hundred per cent.'

I felt that Clive was a sincere and honest man and he believed the regressions were genuine memories of previous lives. But, as a Buddhist seeking to renounce the world and its mistaken values, my world view and his were sometimes at odds. However I had to follow these regressions according to his Christian values and could not expect him to speak from a Buddhist point of view. Clive was a great romantic; for him the story of Yukio and her lord was a great love story, in a way it was a love story but the rules of engagement were very different and much stricter than our modern interpretation of romantic love. In spite of that, I can agree that it was a great romance as it could not have stood the ravages of time without a passionate heart.

And when they were separated at the end of her life, Clive wanted them to be reunited in the shining realms after death. According to my Buddhist belief when this life ends the continuity of this physical body ends. There is no longer anyone or anything to cling to. Our possessions, family and friends of this life are gone forever and we will go alone into our next life empty-handed; we can only take with us the good and bad potentials left on our minds at the end of this life.

Although I needed to answer Clive's questions here, I knew that going to revisit my past life held no meaning for me; as a Buddhist I was secretly pleased that I had lost interest in that life.

Buddhists are taught not to develop attachment to people and possessions as this will prevent them from having the ability to free themselves or others from life's problems.

Someone who lives peacefully and harmoniously throughout their life as Yukio did is more likely to die with a happy and peaceful mind.

When Yukio's consciousness left her body and floated up above the cold forest of leafless trees, I realised with relief that her feelings of cold, hunger and loneliness ended as soon as that life had ended. The peace and comfort she then experienced could not be compared with the most wonderful experiences of this life.

Chapter 8

JUST OLD COLD BONES

Morning meditation over, I had a few minutes to relax and have breakfast with my friends before catching the train to White Lodge where I was to take part in a healing course on colour therapy.

For several years I had dreamed of writing a book on colour as a healing tool. Not that I knew much about it, I just knew it worked and I loved colour. Soon my understanding should improve.

I arrived at the lodge after several hours on a train and met my fellow students: two Spanish men, a gentleman from London, an Australian acupuncturist and the two ladies who were to share a room with me. The Spanish men demanded a private locked room as they had a collection of precious and semi-precious healing stones. We were shown around the sanctuary which included a chapel, a classroom and a colour room, which reminded me of an arcade full of slot machines. Each carousel had letters from people who wanted to be healed suspended on spokes radiating out from the centre, and which revolved slowly under appropriate coloured lights. There was the broken bone carousel where letters from people who had broken their bones were suspended; the heart carousel and the cancer carousel, as well as many others. They all moved gently and silently around under their respective coloured lights in the dimly lit room. I was reminded of an amusement arcade but felt it inappropriate to point this out; so I watched the spectacle silently with the rest of the group. Who was I to say that this method of healing was ineffective?

Each morning we arrived in the classroom for our instruction. I was very impressed with Peter, a psychometrist. Taking something from each of us in turn and holding the object in his hand, he could then tell us something about our life which was to help us in the future. After telling me about a couple of traumatic experiences in my childhood, the first when I was a toddler and the second when I was seven.

Then I was simply told that I was a wonderful mother. But I did wonder how I deserved such praise.

The following day Alan taught us the theory of colour therapy and advised us that if we wished to qualify as colour therapists we must follow his instructions closely when we wrote our thesis. I was an attentive student and my thesis, which I sent them a few months later, earned me a pass.

There was certainly an unusual energy around this lodge. That evening I went up to my room to meditate alone. Absorbed in meditation after the busy day's instruction, and enjoying the peace and quiet of the empty room, I was startled by the plumbing that rumbled when someone turned on a tap nearby. A minute later, one of the Spanish men knocked on the door to ask if I was alright. It was true I had jumped out of my skin when the plumbing rattled unexpectedly, but how did he know? I don't think I made a sound to indicate my fright.

I have no doubt colour heals, especially coloured light. I have read this had been discovered during the war, when the doctors treating wounded soldiers noticed they recovered faster when placed in the sunlight which shone through the stained glass windows of the churches that were used as temporary hospitals, proving stained glass is not just attractive but also has healing power. Perhaps the images of Saints and Holy men also played a part in the healing process.

I was glad I had come on this course but was not at ease among the quiet coloured lights. It seemed a rather materialistic form of other worldly healing.

On the last day, I had planned to leave early and go to visit my family in Hastings. But the course organisers insisted I had to stay for the final session in the afternoon. This was to be held in the chapel. Finally I gave in and after a vegetarian lunch, we found our way to the chapel where seven chairs were placed facing each other with our names on them. A lady entered in a long purple ball gown that had seen better days and some old men appeared. It seemed as if they had seeped in through the solid walls but possibly there were doors with curtains.

Alan went and stood behind the first chair and, after making the sign of the cross on the man's forehead, he laid his hands on the man's shoulders, and made some predictions which were recorded and sent on later. I was third and after the cross had been made on my brow with his thumb, he began …

I remember I was dancing in the deserts of time but the rest is now forgotten, buried in the sand. After everyone had received their message the mediums left without a word and we followed them out into the bright autumn sunlight, and went home.

I boarded the train in Tonbridge, and as it rattled towards Hastings I contemplated my good fortune. I was happy I was going to visit Paula and my family, happy I was a Buddhist and glad I had attended this course. But sorry that someday I would not be able to see the beautiful colour of Buddhas or butterflies wings any more.

Butterfly beautiful; yellow, bright,
Spreading joy throughout the day,
Where ever you alight.

Sinking further down into my seat on the warm train, to pass the time I contemplated my Buddhist path.

When I began reading about Buddhism and then became interested in the Buddhism of Tibet, I had discovered that many of the images of Buddhas not only had extra arms and heads but also that each one was a different colour. Tara was green; Manjushri the Buddha of wisdom was orange and Avalokiteshvara was white and had one thousand arms. Why were they coloured? Why lots of arms? There were also red and blue Buddhas, but perhaps I should stop being so literal and just accept these images which I could find no reasonable explanation for, but which I had been told were capable of blessing my mind and healing me if I visualised them in front of me and recited their mantras. But for this meditation to work I would need strong faith and a good imagination, and not expect quick results.

First I was instructed to visualise a Buddha in front of me; for example the blue coloured Medicine Buddha, and then, while contemplating his special attributes and reciting his mantra, I was to imagine blue lights and nectars flowing down into my body and mind.

According to Buddhism, each colour has a different healing power. Some filled my mind with the light of wisdom while others, such as the green light of Tara protected me from fear and danger.

This reminded me of the wounded soldiers I had heard of lying on their beds with light streaming down from the images of the saints in the stained glass windows in the churches used as hospitals during the war Perhaps each saint healed in a different way?

Also, it is not so far removed from the Catholic belief that Saint Christopher, the patron saint of travellers, would protect them on their journeys if they wore an image of him around their neck. Or that Saint Anthony could help us find something we had lost if we prayed to him. How many faithful Catholics would deny the healing power of Our Lady of Lourdes? As a Catholic I had never questioned the healing power of saints, so why should I now have any problem accepting the healing power of Buddhas?

As the train trundled south, I continued my reverie.

From the perspective of one hundred years why should I be concerned about the trivial ups and downs of this one short life? Surely what I should be doing is finding a way to give my life a meaning that will outlast the death of my body?

Why am I not constantly aware of my mortality? Obviously because I do not want to dwell on it. However my teacher recommends that each day I remind myself that I may die today. Why? Because if I am aware of how precarious my life is I will also see how precious it is and rather than waste it I will try to live every day in a meaningful way. And after all who can say with certainty that they will not die today? Often it is only when we realise that something will come to an end that we can begin to value it. How many people come to appreciate their friends and possessions after they have lost them? This life is a wonderful gift, but won't last forever. When I can take to heart the fact that my life could end anytime, I hope I will not continue to waste it on meaningless pursuits, but instead treat it as a priceless gift from my parents.

To remind myself of this I occasionally tell myself that within this very body there is already a skeleton. In one hundred years I will be a skeleton of course; but I am already a skeleton right now, just wrapped in flesh and skin; hidden from view and out of sight.

If I practice Buddhism purely now, my life will be much more interesting; I will make right choices and as a result, create happiness for myself and others, this will create the potential to be happier in future lives. Death-awareness is not depressing or morbid; instead it causes us to see the true value of our present life. When we can appreciate every moment of this life we will make right choices now and in the future.

I need to develop a greater interest in my future lives as they will last far longer than this one short life. From this perspective I will not get upset with life's trivial annoyances.

As a child I had been taught that I had to be a good girl, but I had never heard of the possibility of going beyond this point. Jesus was the shepherd and I was a sheep. Although I *love* sheep, and the wild hills in Cumbria where they live, I now know that as a Buddhist I do not have to be a sheep. With great effort I can become a shepherd, a Buddha. Maybe not in this life, but in one of my lives to come.

How does Buddhist life compare to Christian life? As a Buddhist I can follow the graduated path to enlightenment known as Lam rim in Tibetan. Of course it is not a journey up a hill or mountain; it is a journey of the mind from confusion to everlasting happiness. This systematic and graduated path was composed by Atisha. It shows the aspirant how to progress step by step from where they are now, a very limited and self-centred person, into a fully enlightened Buddha with limitless compassion, wisdom and spiritual power.

Throughout my Catholic education the idea of being able to progress or even the need to progress had not been explained. The emphasis had been on not slipping back rather than going forward. But the idea of creating my own future was exciting and challenging.

The week I spent in Hastings with Paula passed quickly and when it came to an end I had to travel back to Manjushri Institute. After morning meditation I came out of the dark cool cloisters and into the dazzling sunlight with a cup of tea. My friends were still sitting on the wall opposite the main door and it seemed to me they had not moved since I left to go south the week before. But in my absence they had transformed the chapel into a café which would be open to tourists in time for the Easter holidays and throughout the summer season.

Jean, my friend and neighbour was sitting on the wall watching a small caterpillar walking slowly away when I joined her. I asked her why she thought people disliked caterpillars but liked butterflies. This was a mystery to me; after all they were the same insect, just in a different stage of development. People spray poison on their plants to kill caterpillars but who would kill a beautiful butterfly? These same people would even buy seeds to make a butterfly garden, but would seeds for a caterpillar garden sell so well?

Jean's reply was interesting. She said she thought people should look at each moment as a link in a chain rather than an isolated event. If we did this our behaviour would change. We would love caterpillars as much as butterflies and make them gardens too. Certainly we would view our human life very differently if we saw it as a link in a long, long chain. Normally we take it for granted that human beings are superior and more important than caterpillars, but if our lives are like links in a chain, who is to say that one link is more important than another? Perhaps in a previous life I was an insect, and perhaps in a future life I will be one again.

The sun had now gone behind the clouds and the morning air was getting damp and chilly. My friends had left to begin their day's work so I got up from the wall and walked quickly towards my flat.

As I approached the door I thought about our

discussion and remembered the words of the lady in the blue coat who I had met while sitting on the same wall last summer: *'There is so much love in the world!'*

But as a child I had caught caterpillars and butterflies because I loved them. Then I had trapped them in jars for the remainder of their short lives. Would Jean still want to be my friend if she knew? In a way I had loved them; but not in the right way. I have heard karma described as good fortune and even good luck. But of course this good luck has arisen from our collective past good and bad actions. The caterpillars and butterflies had very bad luck to have met me as an ignorant child.

The following morning was bright and clear and I wanted to spend some time quietly by the bay before the day began.

Going down to the bay, I sat on a small grassy knoll for my breakfast picnic. Looking across to the distant hills I drank my tea and thought about yesterday's discussion.

In fact I am one of those people who do like caterpillars although I do not wish to be one. I also remembered my brother David and I playing in the Lyndhurst garden on an insect safari, and catching flies at the nursery window.

Now I knew more about the life of a fly. I knew they had a right to life just as I did and that just as I felt pain when I was hurt, so did they. But as a child these little beings had not been welcome in our house, and although we did not spray them, Dad would kill them by swatting them on the walls. Had I been brought up as a Buddhist then I would have known that deliberately killing even a tiny insect was wrong; and I would have been taught to respect all forms of life.

But thinking about the law of karma I realised I had no one but myself to blame, through my own ignorance and cruelty in previous lives I had created the cause to be born into a culture where insect killing was encouraged.

I walked back through the woods in the late summer sunshine for the first instruction of the day. As I walked, I listened to the flies buzzing high up in the branches of the trees. Although each one was so small and could only emit a tiny sound, collectively they made the treetops hum and the sound of humming flies took on a new dimension. Without the flies the birds would go hungry; and without the flies the sweet sound of late summer would be silenced forever.

I found a spare cushion to sit on in the crowded room. The morning's instruction was about to begin.

While waiting for the teacher to enter I now remembered I had another way to still attachment, which works well. I simply ask myself, 'What will be important in one hundred years? Will it be the beautiful voice or unpleasant sound of this person's speech?'

Then during my meditation I brought to mind the voice of Barry, my first boyfriend, that voice that I found so exciting to listen to. But that same voice was the one that had rejected me in favour of another girl. How could one voice be the cause of so much happiness but finally the cause of unbearable pain when the sound of his voice had hit me like poison arrows and broken my teenage heart? If the pleasure that had arisen from this friendship was really true then the fire of my teenage love could never be extinguished. If the ashes of resentment continued to smoulder deep inside me, they would re-ignite again, unless I had poured the cool water of forgiveness over them.

If I fail to forgive before I die, the smouldering embers of teenage passion would re-ignite fanned by the wind of attachment until they became an uncontrollable forest fire. There can be no greater Hell than a heart ablaze with unrequited teenage love.

So now during my meditation I can imagine that one hundred years have passed. My friends are all gone; all that remains of them are skeletons, like the one that is beneath my own flesh and skin. So what is there to be attached to? What sense is there in clinging to people who so soon will become a bunch of old, cold bones?

Buddha taught that when we are reborn we will re-enact the dramas of this life if we do not make a great effort to overcome them now. Our name and place of birth may be different, but our attitudes will not change unless we make a conscious effort to change them ourselves right now.

Do I really want to re-enact the same old stories of passion betrayal and loss, over and over again?

Or would I rather be someone who had overcome attachment to life and left pain and passion behind? This is the time to transform passion into compassion, but I also need to develop wisdom and never forget we are just old, cold bones.

Chapter 9

THE LILY AND THE LOTUS

Beth was on her lunch break and asked if I would like to go for a walk through the woods to the bay with her.

As we made our way along the overgrown path I noticed it was edged with tiny flowers of every colour which could be seen through watchful eyes. Bright yellow tormentil hugged the ground and contrasted with the scarlet pimpernel and bright blue speedwell which hid shyly under the shady trees by the path. The old tree trunks were graced with garlands of red and white campion and dark green nettles, which gave way to the soft creamy clusters of meadowsweet as we approached the pond, where a little moorhen darted over the still surface of the water towards the ducks.

Beth, who was an artist, wanted to draw the trees, but I was lost in the colours, sounds and smells which confronted me on every side.

Suddenly she stopped my train of thought by asking why the Buddhas sat on a lotus when they could sit on a rose in full bloom. She was painting a picture of a Buddha, and felt that a rose would be prettier than a lotus in her painting. This was a new idea to me. A lotus is not a native plant to England and belongs to the East, not the West.

While we sometimes had lilies in our ponds, I had never seen a lotus except in a painting. Thinking about this there did seem to be some valid reason for depicting Buddha seated on a rose instead of a lotus.

My mother had said that the lily was a symbol of purity, which is why St. Joseph is portrayed as holding a bunch of lilies. But these white lilies are the ones which grow in soil, and not on lakes in England and are to be seen in Catholic Churches at Easter.

However the lotus is also a symbol of purity. A lotus has its roots in the mud at the bottom of a lake but rises up through the water until the buds burst open to reveal the soft, white velvet petals, untouched by the muddy water. In a similar way we begin our life in the mud of our confused minds and through long years of spiritual growth finally we flower as a completely pure Buddha. The difference between ordinary beings like me and a Buddha is that I am still like a young lotus shoot living in the mud of my delusions, whereas Buddhas have risen up through the mud and transformed into a beautiful flower. Yet we are all capable of becoming lotus blossoms. This is one difference between Buddhism and other religions.

In Christianity, for example, God is the creator and we are created beings; through spiritual practice we can draw closer to God but we can never become God. We can never stop being a created being and become the Creator.

Beth left me satisfied that although a rose would be pretty, it would not have the same depth of meaning as a lotus. I couldn't help wondering, though, whether the beautiful white lilies that St. Joseph had held in his arms had originally had exactly the same meaning, but over the centuries the reason why the lily represented purity was completely forgotten.

After Beth had returned happily to paint Buddha sitting on a lotus and I had started work in my flat, there was a knock on the back door and I opened it to find my neighbour Aunt Sue standing unsteadily in the doorway.

She hadn't been drinking – the unsteady gait came from her considerable years and her inappropriate high heels. She had come from New York and had moved into the flat next to mine. Not understanding the electricity meter, she had overfilled it once again, causing it to cut out. We needed to get it reset before it got cold and dark.

I had become used to these little problems over the years. This delightful old lady, whom everyone called 'Aunt Sue,' had in fact only one nephew in England. She was a lady who had been old for a very long time, and as she was my closest neighbour frequently needed my attention. Coming from New York, she had lied about her age so many times, that by now she had genuinely forgotten how old she was herself.

She was so stiff she could hardly move, and so deaf she could hardly hear, but she was a typically tough New Yorker and had the courage to come to England to be near her nephew Chip. Each day was a struggle and getting harder, but she bore it bravely. Her city wardrobe was completely inappropriate for the north west of England, but she was too fixed in her ways to change.

The electricity back on again, we decided to go to town for afternoon tea. Putting on her best old coat and squashing her feet painfully into her neat little city shoes, she wrapped her pretty rose coloured scarf about her neck to keep out the cold, and we took a taxi into town. Shopping was a nightmare for both of us. Our English market town shops were very different to the New York department stores she was accustomed to, but the shopkeepers were very patient, making allowances for her deafness and stiffness by shouting slowly and loudly while finding the items she needed. She only had real problems when she could not translate what she wanted from New York English to Cumbrian English. Here we eat coffee cake, but her coffee cake was different to ours; usually she got more or less what she wanted before we returned home.

127

(Aunt) Sue McGee was a sincere Catholic and, not having any brothers or sisters to share the task, she had spent all of her young adult life caring for two sick and bedridden parents as well as looking after the family business.

When they died she found herself middle-aged, alone and unmarried. By then she was so used to caring for others she continued by caring for her young relatives. I did not wish for Paula to have a similar life, and find herself middle-aged and alone. So, although I missed Paula greatly, I was happy she was able to live in Hastings, with her Uncle David and Aunty Pat, far away from me but sharing in a real family life and getting on with her own, rather than being trapped into looking after her disabled mother.

But this tough, old New Yorker had always put herself last and to all who knew her she was just Aunt Sue.

Suffering was her daily lot, but she accepted it with courage and a great sense of humour. We spent hours discussing her early life and exchanging our views on anything that came to mind; my life was much richer for having spent time with her. She belonged to a different time and culture and her stories were always fascinating, her world so different to mine.

As her health deteriorated she needed more care and it fell upon me to make and share supper with her each night. During these evening meals she told me about her mother whom she had loved dearly and was her closest friend. Her mother had died on Easter Monday many years earlier, and Sue had decided never to burden anyone by spending her last years in bed being cared for by others. She knew better than anyone how onerous such a task could be. Even so, I have to say that before she became bed-ridden herself she was quite a handful and a trial of my patience.

When she slipped on her bathroom floor she called for me to help and, as she was a Catholic, the parish organised for me to get a lift to the hospital to visit.

I found her in a corner of the ward giving orders to the young male nurse, and went to sit by her bed and chat. As we chatted, the man from the Catholic charity who had offered me the lift ran his fingers up and down my spine. Not understanding the etiquette in such an unconventional situation, and not wanting to upset Sue by making a scene, I continued chatting and ignored him until he tired and went off to visit another sick lady.

After she recovered from her fall, she returned home to her flat and to her sometimes eccentric lifestyle. There was only one way to do anything. Her way!

During Easter week the weather was perfect, warm and sunny. Everyone seemed to have gone on holiday and the flats were almost deserted; the bay glinted in the bright sunlight and a gentle breeze moved softly through the tops of the trees. Easter could not get any better. After the long, cold winter bright green shoots were waking up to the promise of summer days.

But Sue's health was failing and when she became ill again I called the doctor, who wanted her to go into hospital immediately as she now needed 24-hour care. I knew Sue was afraid of hospital, so I offered to stay with her overnight; this satisfied the doctor and he left.

Easter Sunday, again the weather was perfect, bright and sunny. Some friends came and brought her a massive bunch of daffodils and sat at her bedside chatting until she became very weak and unable to speak clearly.

When the doctor returned she said, 'I know I am dying as Philippa has called my nephew.'

Later that afternoon she said to me, 'I have urinated for the last time.'

I knew she was right, but could not find the words to reply, so said nothing. But will I have such presence of mind on my last day on earth?

She chatted a little and, reviewing her life, she said in her wonderful New York drawl, 'I never married, I am still a virgin, but I don't think I've missed anything.'

A naughty little smile lit up her drawn pale face. 'I am going to go to the Catholic Heaven not the Buddhist Heaven.'

And it occurred to me that such a determined and pure-spirited lady would not have to worry about sitting on a lotus there but she certainly did deserve some white lilies.

The rest of the day was spent in instructing me in the art of making perfect chicken soup, which she called Jewish penicillin, as she said that in New York the Jewish community made chicken soup when they were ill. Then in the early hours of Easter Monday, she quietly passed away.

Was it mere coincidence that her Mother, who she always called her best friend, had also died on Easter Monday? Is there a more wonderful or meaningful way for a good Catholic to die? Such remarkable presence of mind. Such a truly brave and selfless lady. I hope she found her Heaven and the happiness she deserved.

Chapter 10

THE STONE MAN

The next regression therapy, which took place in May nineteen eighty-seven, took me back to an isolated valley, similar to a Cumbrian valley but on an enormous scale. Looking down at the valley bottom, the river which had created it was just a tiny silver thread meandering lazily over the rocky floor, twisting and turning as it glinted in the bright sun on its way to join an unknown ocean.

I could feel the time passing as Clive gently encouraged me to describe the area.

'What can you see?'

I could see the sunlit valley but I could also hear the lambs bleating outside the window of this Cumbrian house. Two lives divided by time and distance, but equally valid. As I lay in the shady room I was aware of Clive and the chatter from the kitchen but at the same time I was far away in this sunlit valley. Unlike in a dream, I could be guided by Clive and the experience was closer to a movie than a dream. Clive was the director but I was in charge of casting, costumes and props.

Clive asked me again what I could see. I explained I was a small, old man dressed in a rough reddish brown hooded cloak that covered my body from head to foot. I was walking alone uphill with the help of a stick which I held in my left hand for support on the long and steep ascent up the right side of the valley. I must have walked for hours and there did not seem to be any sign of life, either human or animal; just long grass and cloudless, clear blue sky. It was cool at this great height but the sun was powerful.

Although I can recount this story quite quickly, when Clive prompted me it was difficult and sometimes I was silent for several minutes while he coaxed me to speak. Perhaps it was because I was suspended between both lives. Although I knew I was in the room with Clive at all times and was aware of my body lying on the bed and the warm air of the room, I was unaware of *Philippa* as such.

Clive patiently led me through this regression as I hesitantly explained in a soft squeaky voice what I saw. I still wondered how the car-salesman had become this healer who was asking my higher-self to find a past life that would be relevant to my health in this life and in particular to my poor vision.

When I turned a corner on the mountainside and a cave appeared before me, I could sense Clive's discomfort. What could he ask about this boring little man who walked up a mountain? Why was this life so important?

As the sparrows tweeted outside the window and lambs called to their mothers in the nearby fields, Clive asked me about the cave.

'Are you going to visit someone or do you live there?'

Again I could sense Clive's unease as he continued to encourage me to explore the meaning of this past life.

'Tell me all that you experience there. You said that it was a cave on a precipice.'

Finally I approached the dark entrance and went inside, I concluded that it could be a hermitage.

Now Clive asked about the old man's hair, I found the question funny and, laughing a little, I said that, as the man wore a hood, I did not know the colour of his hair or eyes.

In the silence it occurred to me that Clive was a good man, patient and kind, but I was still a little uncomfortable with him. After deciding that I was about fifty, which was possibly Clive's age, I described the man. He was short, and quite broad. Clive asked if there was some specific reason for my going there. I explained to Clive I was there to do a retreat and had to remain in the cave for a certain length of time.

'Why?'

'To attain some deeper understanding.'

'Of anything in particular?'

In an almost inaudible whisper, 'Of life.'

'Do you belong to some religious order, or are you an initiate?'

I have been advised by someone to go to this cave for a certain length of time.

'Who has advised you?'

'A religious person. You get advice from religious people. If you find someone with more experience than you, then you can ask them to give you some instruction. After that you must go away and try and understand what they have told you. This can take a long time. It is not an organised religion.' (It crossed my mind that although Clive was a Christian, his style of religion could hardly be described as organised either.)

There are just a lot of individual people who are trying to gain some understanding of the meaning of life.

'Of the meaning of life?'

'Yes, of life and how to overcome suffering.'

'How to overcome suffering? And has there been much suffering in your life?'

'There is suffering in everybody's life'

'But are you aware of specific areas in your own where there has been suffering?'

After a long pause … 'I am aware I am not satisfied with life or the values that people have.'

'So you sought the guidance or advice of one of these spiritual teachers? And he suggested you came up to this retreat to find life's deeper meaning?'

'Yes.'

'Do you know what he told you?'

After another long pause, I say I can see my Tibetan teacher of this present life, with his horn rimmed glasses on, nodding and smiling and saying, 'Oh, this is very good!'

'I see.'

I was amused at Clive's concern about the intrusion of my teacher of this present life into a past life regression. I repeated, 'He looks very pleased.'

Again Clive said, 'I see.' But I suspected he did not see.

'Do you know what part of the world you are living in?'

'I'm not sure.'

'Is it England?'

'No, not England.'

'Then much to Clive's alarm, I explained that sometimes people walled themselves into these caves.

Now Clive sat up very straight and asked 'How would they do that?'

I noticed the entrance of the cave was now walled up. I could not be sure whether I or some other person had built the wall, but there it was, and I was sitting inside facing a dark wall.

I answered Clive, 'Probably by getting someone to build a wall out of stone.'

'Is that to stop you from leaving or to let others know that there is someone in the cave?'

I tried to explain to Clive that some people with high spiritual attainments want to give up life in this world before they actually die. They renounce all contact with others and deprive themselves of all sensory pleasures. If they wall themselves in they can meditate undistractedly for many years. When eventually people come and take down the wall they find just a skeleton sitting in meditation posture, their finger nails having grown around their bodies several times like hoops. (I had previously seen a picture of this in a book).

Now the eloquent Clive was lost for words.

'But how do they eat?'

'They don't need to eat.'

'So where do they get their energy from?'

'They get it from …' I hesitated as I felt Clive's unease and sought for an explanation that he might be comfortable with. But there was no easy way to explain this. 'They have yogic powers.'

'I see.'

To make Clive feel better I explained that sometimes they eat stones. They absorb the minerals from stones.

'Is that what you are going to do?' asked Clive in alarm. 'Are you going to be walled in and survive by consuming stones?'

'It seems I have no ambition in this life to do anything except go to this cave.'

Clive, clearing his throat and completely out of his comfort zone, asked me if sometimes people might specify a time when the wall might be removed.

'Yes.'

'Have you done this before?'

'I think I have done retreats before but I don't think I will ever come out of this cave.'

'You won't?'

'No.'

'Do you feel you will stay there until you die?'

'It feels very matter of fact to climb the mountain and enter the cave and stay there. I had been aware of the colours and the scenery on the way up the mountain and of how beautiful and restful it was. I am aware that I have brought no provisions. I've only got the clothes I am wearing. I don't mind.'

'And will you bother to feed yourself?'

The answer came almost like a contented sigh, 'No. I don't think I intend to eat. There are nettles, but I don't think I will eat them.'

Clive now changed the subject, 'The view is quite spectacular I believe, and you have not been to this particular place before?'

'No.'

'But you just feel that you want to stay there. Why do you feel you are just going to die there at the age of fifty, as that is not old for a man?'

'Um … It's hard to explain. I have no worldly ambitions left. I am not very impressed with the values of human beings.'

'So you are aware you have come up here to die?'

'To leave the world of the heavy flesh anyway, yes. Dying is a funny word. I don't think you get lonely in caves.'

'No, I am sure you don't. Why do you think that is?'

'I think when you abandon the values of the world you realise the people who you see are very transitory; then you get in touch with other beings, higher beings, and they look after you.'

Now Clive spoke with great feeling, 'Yes, I understand that. So you don't have to worry about loneliness. And do you get in touch with these higher beings?'

'Yes.'

'How long do you stay there?'

We both listened with interest as this little life's drama unfolded, 'I am not sure; it is a very long time.'

'And these higher beings you get in touch with, do they appear to you on the inner planes? Or do they actually come into the physical plane?'

There was a long pause punctuated by the chirping of sparrows outside the bedroom window. Clive prompted me again, 'During your long periods of meditation what do you sense about these higher beings?'

In the long silences I sought for answers to Clive's questions.

'Colour!'

'What colour do you notice?'

'Lots of colours!'

'What sort of colours do you see?'

'Red and blue.'

'And do you find peace, an inner peace, a serenity with the divine?'

'I don't think they communicate with my physical body. I think I have a blue body.'

'A blue body!'

'It can only be seen by those who have a similar body.'

'I see. '

'I can see my body it looks very heavy. It looks like a stone.'

Now Clive spoke directly to the stone man, asking him what secret he held that was clouding his friend's eyesight.

'What connection has this man with Philippa's eyesight? Is it the manner in which he dies? Although I know you don't like the word death or dying. Shall we say it is the manner which the …'

At this point I interrupted, 'Transference.'

'Yes, the heavy body separates from the etheric body. And has this caused some impairment of the senses? I am obviously addressing this question to your higher consciousness, for we don't see any obvious connection. Did anything happen or take place that was not planned - anything that has caused an overlap of negative energy?'

In the silence Clive asked me (Philippa) if I was sensing or searching to pick anything up. This was tiring and answers were often hard to find.

'I can see the heavy body, just sitting. It looks like a

rock.'

'Have you still got that cape on?'

'It seems to have. It seems that the wall is blocking out the light but it is still light enough to see. The body sits very still and never moves, but the consciousness can come in and out through the head.'

'I see.'

'It is just like a house, a house for the consciousness.'

'And it is not being fed?'

'No it's not being fed and it's not decaying. It does not even breathe, it's like a stone.'

'Will you move a little closer to this rock-like body and look at the face, especially at the eyes? What do you see there?' Now I noticed he was made of stone and his body was covered in dust from countless years of sitting in that cave alone.

Clive was uncomfortable with this life and I was too. It was very strange.

'It is very hard to see the face and eyes.'

'Why is that?'

'Well, the eyes are closed. It just looks like the body is made of rock.'

'Have the eyes been closed for a long time?'

'They must have been; there's dust covering the whole body and the eyes.'

Clive asked me what else I knew about this man. But there was little to say.

'So it seems that the eyes are almost asleep but the consciousness is still coming in and out of the body. Is there any time when this identification with the body ceases and the spirit or soul never reoccupies the body?'

'Yes.'

'Is there a big transition from that point on?'

I could feel Clive eager to understand this rather

unconventional regression. Where was it going? My replies dripped out of my mind slowly and through my lips.

'The body stays the same as if it were made of rock. It is like occupying a body whose eyes are perpetually closed. '

It is as if the sense of sight has closed down a long time ago, even though the consciousness is still using that body. This is very strange.'

'Even if your physical eyes were open or closed in this cave it would make no difference as it is too dark. There is no light at all. But it doesn't matter because there is spiritual light.'

'That may be fine for the consciousness and for the spiritual body but I would think most unhealthy for the physical body. Do you think you chose this life because of a deeply held belief that the physical body is of no importance whatsoever? I am bound to wonder, what is the point of having a physical body in the first place?'

I was impressed with Clive's effort to grasp such an unusual rebirth without criticism. Even though it was so difficult for him to understand and must have conflicted with some of his values.

In an effort to help him understand my own Buddhist view I told him, 'We need a physical body, and in particular a human body, in order to overcome suffering. Human beings suffer more than other beings. Non-physical beings don't suffer in the same way. They are often so content, they don't develop the wish to overcome suffering. They live in a sort of suspended state where whatever they want appears as soon as they think of it. In contrast human beings are suffering either mentally or physically almost constantly.

'Do you still think that it is necessary to have a physical body?'

'Yes you do need a physical body because that is the

142

source of the five senses.'

Without the five senses there is no relationship between the self and other things. If you can't see, hear, touch, smell, or taste then there is no relationship between you and anything else. It is only through the five senses that it is possible for a human being to interact with anything else.

'Without the five senses there would not be the corresponding awareness of things on higher planes either?'

'There would be an awareness of things on the higher planes. But on the higher planes as soon as you want something you get it. So you are not aware that you can aspire to anything better. The desires of your higher plane body are instantly fulfilled. But with a human body desire is very rarely instantly fulfilled, whether it is for food or anything else. So it is only in the human realm that you can overcome desire. I also have the impression that in the higher realms there is a sense of equality, so there is no jealousy or competitiveness. But this means that you can't overcome something like jealousy in the higher realms if it does not exist there. You need to be in the human realm to do this.'

'Do you feel there has been some overlap or overshadow that is clouding your sense of sight? Perhaps because your physical body was in the dark for so long even though it was still visited from time to time by your subtle body. Do you feel that this is clouding your vision?'

'Most of my senses are slightly dimmed.'

'If you sit in a dark cave every day, week after week, month after month, then you are hardly going to touch anything either are you? Or be touched. So you are de-sensitising the whole of the body.'

'De-sensitising the physical body, yes, but on a

higher plane you can also smell, taste, touch, hear, and see.'

'Of course, but you should understand that my brief here is to find the cause of any impairment or deterioration in sensitivity of the physical body that is lying on this bed.'

At this point I was getting frustrated with Clive's insistence on seeing the face and felt there may be many more interesting aspects of this life that I would like to explore. 'I don't understand why I could not see the person from the front, but only from the back. I have not seen the face clearly and I don't know anything about the man's life before he began walking up the mountain.- Perhaps there were other aspects of his life to understand but I was powerless to do more than respond to Clive's questions and his effort to comprehend this strange life was impressive.

Now Clive continued, 'We know that in the deeper senses time has no meaning, so something that happened three thousand years ago is just as potent as something that happened three minutes ago, because in the deeper consciousness everything is equally now. The deeper consciousness has absorbed experiences like a massive sponge and what has been absorbed can always be tuned into, like a pilot light that is on all of the time and can at any moment activate fully detailed memories. When we are born each cell gets imprinted with memories, like a kind of genetic code, but one that comes from our past lives rather than from our parents. In this way each cell of your body is coded to operate in a certain way. When this man went into retreat his physical body became almost like stone and his physical senses weakened to almost nothing. Could Philippa's body in some way be relating to this now?

'I know that quite a lot of you advocate that what he did was right for him, and I can even accept this. But I don't think it is right for Philippa. I don't think she wants her body to be operating at half of its potential efficiency. She wants her senses to be one hundred per cent efficient. So what I am saying is that although it was right for him to go into the dark, if something of this is being transmitted through the psychic link and is clouding Philippa's etheric body, then this is something that we need to clear, don't we?'

I agreed with Clive; but secretly I wondered if I meant no.

Clive continued, 'And we can clear it by asking you to shift your awareness a little further away from Philippa's, by moving out of the gravitational field of her earth, as it were, so that her senses and yours are no longer integrated in any way. We are asking for a separation of energy, not of love. Do you understand?'

'Yes.'

'Could you please tell us how you made that transition into the shining realm, and as you do so please allow all of your awareness, all of your energy, to move out of Philippa's physical plane entirely and into the spiritual realms which you were aspiring to...'

(And which I, Philippa, am also aspiring to. But preferably without living in a cave.)

'So could you tell us please what it was like when your life consciousness was no longer integrated in any way with that shell or rock that was once a human body? Would you tell me please about these shining planes, these planes of light? Can you see reality now from the shining planes? This would be helpful and healing for Philippa. If you can just relate through her now from that level so that there is no echo coming through the psychic system between you. You are probably laughing at me now, thinking how complicated I make this sound. I know we tend to complicate things on this physical plane. But I think

145

you know what I am trying to achieve, and what Philippa wants to achieve.'

Now the stone man spoke, expressing what he thought of Philippa's limited view of his experience. With obvious disapproval the stone man explained that her view was coloured by a book that she had read some years earlier. 'She thinks that I should look like a skeleton rather than like a stone because that's her expectation of a body in decay.'

Clive now spoke to the stone man directly, 'But to her, even though she is an esoteric person, the state that you were in - of living in your body and yet being outside it - is alien to the kind of world that Philippa lives in now, where she does need to have a particularly sharp sense of vision, hearing, smell, taste and touch, because in the world that she lives in she is seeing and hearing, touching and tasting all of the time. Rather than de-sensitise, she wants to increase her sensory powers. So your etheric envelope that's been around her own like several layers of skin is an impediment to her senses. You are simply on two very different paths.

(I secretly hoped that I was not on such a different path although I did want to have good eyesight.)

Clive continued, 'Whereas you wanted to let the body turn to stone, letting the senses gradually wind down, she wants to live fully in her physical body with sharp senses.'

At this point, I noticed a small red lady rather like a tiny fairy came and hovered above the stone man's head. Holding out her hand, she called and through the crown of the man's head appeared a small blue man. As I watched, she reached out her hand to him and grasping his hand in hers flew up into the clear blue sky. He had been residing at the heart of the stone man, but had been free to come and go like a bird in a nest; just like the red lady, he was made of clear light

146

and was not obstructed by the man's rock-like body nor walls of the cave. While the stone man sat immobile.

I explained to Clive, 'A red lady came to get my blue body and take it by the hand.'

'A red lady came to take your blue body and take it by the hand. How beautiful. Where did she take you?'

'Up.'

'Up to the higher planes of being?'

'Yes.'

'I've never heard the bodies of the soul described so vividly in colour before. As you have such a greatly developed sense of colour will you now from your shining planes help Philippa also to have a greater sense of colour and a greater sense of light? Will you help her to open her vision more and more so that she need not see the world through a dark tunnel, or a cave?'

'She knows the red lady.'

'Does she?'

'Yes.'

'In what sense does she know her?'

'She's got to become like her.'

'I'm glad; of course she has. That's what this is all about isn't it? Is there anything else you wish to say now? Don't you wish to give Philippa some advice?'

At this point the red lady did speak to me, but I kept silent and, just like the memory of a dream, I forgot what she said before I left the room; however, I hope it still remains buried somewhere deep in my consciousness.

'No words. Just a state of being and feeling.'

After this regression I went out for a walk along the lakeside road for a mile or so, feeling the need for quiet contemplation.

The evening was drawing in and the rain began to

fall heavily from a leaden sky. Whether I had really been taken back to a previous life seemed to me to be less important than whether it would help me to understand my present life, the one I am living right now. I hoped that the driving rain would wash away my confusion about the regression.

The sky remained overcast and the rain did not stop. As I walked rapidly back to the welcoming lights of Nether Wasdale in the fading light I recalled a local ghost story.

For many years, when people died in the Wasdale valley, coffins had to be carried over the Burnmoor Corpse Road by pack horse to St.Catherine's church in the Eskdale valley, while the mourners followed on foot.

Local legend has it that when carrying the coffin of a young man, on reaching the fell top, the mist descended and the brown horse carrying the coffin suddenly bolted. As it could not be found in the thick mist the funeral party returned home. Shortly after, the young man's mother died of grief and the funeral party once more set out across the corpse road. This time with the mother, on the back of a grey mare.

Again mist descended and the horse galloped off. Soon the mourners found a brown horse with the son's coffin still strapped to its back. However, the grey mare was never seen again. But there are those who have heard hooves beating on the moor when the mist descends.

Feeling chilly, my pace quickened as I hurried back through the mist and rain to the house.

When I got back I was admonished for getting soaked to the skin. So I took off everything I wore, showered and put on dry clothes before going down to supper. I had had a wonderful day doing what no sane person would do.

Three ladies had arrived and after supper we chatted in the lounge. They were regulars and all were Spiritualists; three lovely ladies, not young but with very strong minds. All three were interested in what Buddhists were doing to relieve suffering. As usual they were speaking of the suffering of this life, not of future lives. Three beautiful ladies sent from the Buddha fields to check my practice of Buddhism? What were Buddhists doing about AIDS? About other social problems? They certainly taxed my brain for an hour or so.

As a Buddhist my main wish was to attain enlightenment for the benefit of all. However the place to begin was right here in this room. And from here my aspiration should spread outwards like the rays of the rising sun; spreading further outwards like the morning light brightening up the night sky and heralding the day. Leaving nothing in its wake, the golden light spreading, spreading ever outwards, helping anyone it came into contact with. But of course my job was not to convert these ladies simply to exchange ideas on social problems. I had really enjoyed our discussion and felt that I had learned a lot. I hoped they had also benefited from exchanging ideas.

Of course only a Buddha who is fully enlightened can benefit others perfectly. But with the blessings of my own teacher, I can begin as a trainee Buddha – a Bodhisattva – right now. And at least I can still pray for those who I meet but can't help directly, by holding a thought in my mind, such as, 'May I be able to help these people who are suffering from AIDS.'

Eventually with practice this thought will become powerful enough to benefit those with serious problems like AIDS.

This way through this human life I can, little by little, develop the compassion, wisdom and skill needed to really help others. All the people and situations I encounter during my daily life can help me develop these qualities, which is what makes a human life so valuable. A stone man can't do this.

Perhaps it is true that in a previous life I was a meditator who turned his body into stone, but in this life I was sure this is not what I needed to do.

Several years later I was watching a series of six programmes on the television about research into mummification practices. One of these programmes focused on Japanese mummys and described a strict sect of monks who aspired to purify their bodies and minds to such a degree that they finally chose to be walled into a cave and spend the remainder of their life in deep, solitary meditation. Each day they would ring a bell so that an assistant would know that they were still alive. When the bell stopped ringing they were considered dead.

After some time the assistants and Holy men would open the cave and the successful aspirant would be found sitting upright in a meditation posture with legs crossed, completely transformed into a stone-like mummy. If they were not pure enough in body and mind when they entered the cave, then they would die just like any other person and their body decompose.

There is quite a famous Japanese story that I would like to tell here, though I must confess that my memory is a bit hazy.

There was once a young farmhand who was tending his crops in a field when two drunken samurai set upon him and tried to kill him with their swords. As they were so drunk, he managed to fight them off with his hoe and he killed them both to save his own life. As samurai were considered irreproachable, he knew that although he had acted in self-defence the death penalty awaited him if he was caught. So without even returning home to say goodbye to his wife and child he ran to the nearby monastery for refuge.

The practice of the monks in this monastery was one of purification. Night and day the senior monks purified their minds and bodies with ritual prayers and diet. When they had reached a high level of attainment, they intensified their practice and the chosen monks would do solitary retreat and live on a special diet of grains for several months. This diet was so extreme that after eating three types of grain for such a long time their bodies became emaciated and the flesh shrunken and shrivelled. They also purified their minds with ritual practices and meditation, renouncing all human pleasures and hoped to go to higher realms as a result of this extreme practice.

At a special time of the year the group would assemble on the bank of a lake to begin the final part of their practice. The lake had no wildlife nor plants, as the waters of the lake were filled with the deadly poison arsenic, killing everything that touched it. The monks who had by now purified both body and mind drank a spoonful of the clear blue toxic water as a final purge. This would have killed anyone else.

Now there was no residual matter in their stomach to putrefy, so they were ready to enter a cave to complete their practice alone and in the dark. Each day they would ring a hand bell. When the bell finally stopped ringing, the assistant went away, returning a considerable time later to open the cave and reveal the contents: either a pile of dust or a mummy. Needless to say, our farm hand was successful and his body was self-mummified.

It seems that four or five hundred years ago self-mummification was quite widely practiced in India, China, Tibet and Japan. I do not know which of these places if any this life belonged to, nor can I claim to have remembered my name at that time, but to give this particular regression some more context I will relate a true story I came across on the internet.

In the northern Himalayan state of Himachal Pradesh, The Hindustan Times reported the existence of a 500 year old mummy. It backed up its claim by publishing a picture of a wizened human sitting in a hunched, meditating position draped with a shawl. The mummy, identified as that of monk Sangha Tenzin, was found inside a tomb at Ghuen village in the cold and remote Spiti district of Himachal Pradesh, about 6,000 metres above sea level.

Ghuen villagers have known about the mummy since nineteen seventy-five, when an earthquake struck the region and brought down a part of the tomb. However, due to the remoteness of Ghuen, in a desolate mountainous area close to India's border with China, restricted to the public and under the control of the paramilitary Indo-Tibetan Border Police, the mummy's existence has remained under wraps.

However, a Hindustan Times staffer managed to get access and took photographs of the mummy.

Victor Mair, a consultant scientist at the University of Pennsylvania Museum of Archaeology and Anthropology, was quoted as saying the mummy was at least five hundred years old. According to the report the mummy is remarkably well preserved for its age. Its skin is unbroken and there is hair on its head. Mair said this was partly to do with the extreme cold and dry air of the region.

'Slow starvation in the last few months of his life reduced the body fat and shrunk parts of the body that would have been liable to putrefaction.'

The report did not say where the mummy is now being kept.

Ghuen village is about fifty kilometres from the

Tabo monastery, believed to be the oldest surviving Buddhist establishment in the region. It straddles an ancient trading route through which spices, wool, salt, precious stones and sugar were carried.

At the time of this regression therapy in May nineteen eighty-seven I had never heard of self-mummification, and only when I watched the television series on mummys over ten years later did its significance become apparent.

As a healing tool regression can be very powerful and it gave me great confidence in past and therefore future lives. Obviously my past lives are irretrievably gone, like last night's dream, and there is nothing I can do to change this.

It is not much use learning about our past lives simply out of curiosity, so that we can tell a good story at a party. But when approached with the right attitude, knowing about our past lives definitely has great value.

What I gained from this regression experience is an insight into some of my present attitudes.

In most of the past lives I was taken back to I was illiterate, although in one I was very artistic. Being dyslexic and ambidextrous in this life may possibly be due to being illiterate or belonging to eastern cultures, where apparently writing is done with the opposite side of the brain, the artistic half, where I am always more comfortable.

I might say at this point that I, Philippa, have no wish to become a mummy right now even if I was capable. How can a mummy benefit others?

Chapter 11

RETREAT

I could not conceive of being a Sunday morning Buddhist, a nine to five Buddhist or a part-time Buddhist of any kind. For me it had to be twenty-four seven or nothing, which was easier to say than do.

During the term's teachings in the spring of nineteen eighty-one, Venerable Geshe Kelsang Gyatso said that any Tibetan who was serious about attaining enlightenment would do a retreat of three years at least once in their life. This was what I had been looking for. It was definitely going to be twenty-four seven Buddhism. Was I serious about attaining enlightenment or not? And If I wasn't what was I doing here anyway?

Now all I needed was to find a spare three years.

Paula was still in school and although she was not with me all the time I felt I should wait until she was a little more independent before I took on this commitment.

In the end I waited almost ten years, but if I had not first had the intention to do such a long retreat all those years ago, then when the opportunity finally arose I would not have recognised it, and would probably have spent the three years in some perhaps enjoyable but ultimately meaningless pursuit. Although a three year retreat was still a long way off, I could begin to prepare my mind by becoming familiar with the routine of a retreat. My first opportunity was when Manjushri Institute organised a month long retreat in January nineteen eighty-one, something that became a tradition and has been repeated every year since then.

About twenty people signed up for this first retreat and a large empty room with a wood burning stove was found on the derelict top floor of the building.

We laid out mats and cushions for each person. I found a small table to lay my book and ritual objects upon. Like most other retreaters my 'table' was just an old vegetable box found outside the kitchen, which I covered with a clean red cloth and laid out my prayer book, rosary, and ritual implements. These included a bell and vajra, a small five-pronged object to be held in my right hand whenever I played the bell with my left hand. The bell symbolises emptiness, or ultimate truth, and the vajra symbolises the mind of great bliss. There was also a damaru, a Tibetan hand drum used to invoke the Buddhas. This retreat was a mantra counting retreat, so the most important thing to bring was my rosary or mala, to count the mantras.

One hundred-thousand mantras sounded like an awful lot to me. But reciting so many is a way of coming closer to a particular Tantric Deity. It is like calling their name, or tuning into their special vibration. As we were all new to this practice, Geshe Kelsang had kindly offered to attend the sessions. This was very helpful as I knew nothing about the ritual and could watch as he performed all the mudras, or hand gestures, and try to copy him. The air was filled with the heady smell of incense and excitement as we assembled in the room to begin our retreat, now transformed into a beautiful meditation hall with a richly decorated shrine filled with flowers and pictures of Tantric Deities, the log fire emitting a warm, coniferous glow.

We waited expectantly for Geshe Kelsang to enter. He came quietly into the room and the session began with preliminary prayers and meditation. The rest of the month would follow the same pattern, as we familiarised ourselves with the new practice. Perhaps I sometimes held these strange ritual implements in the wrong hands, but I hoped my heart was in the right place and I thought the Buddhas might be more forgiving of my dyslexia than the Sisters of Mercy had been, as they seemed to think that anyone who went down on the wrong knee when entering the chapel was a child of the devil.

So the first of many of my annual one month retreats had begun. This practice was new to the West and the prayers had not yet been translated into English, so we chanted in Tibetan. The tunes were hauntingly beautiful, but some of the notes not easy to reach and strained my western vocal chords. By the end of the month I was hoarse but happy.

Gradually, over the next few years an English translation was prepared, but it was many years before music that could support the translation was composed, so for now everything was chanted in Tibetan.

Throughout the January retreat, I moved in with my warmest clothing, duvet and flask. The famous hot water toilet, which had been my only source of comfort on my first visit, was very close. Luxury!

The winter was one of the worst in memory. Everything froze up, inside and out. Each morning on my way to the six o'clock session I stopped off to break a thick layer of ice which had formed in the toilets, as a chill breeze blew relentlessly through the missing panes of glass into the unheated bathroom. This little task could be performed quite quickly once I had mastered the technique, by using an upturned mop to crack the ice and then pulling each toilet chain to get the water flowing again. By the end of the retreat I noticed with pride that mine was the only fully functional bathroom in the entire building, the rest had succumbed to frost and ice.

At the end of January came the great thaw. Water

flowed everywhere. Umbrellas were needed inside the cloisters, as water from frozen pipes seeped through the fabric of the building from the top floor down to the basement. There were buckets and basins everywhere to catch the steadily dripping water from the thawing snow on the roof. At this time the building had no functional central heating. After the war Conishead Priory had been used as a Durham Miners rest home, and of course they had access to unlimited fuel for the massive boiler in the basement. But now the radiators stood around cold and idle, and in the years after the miners left and before the Buddhists arrived the building had fallen into disrepair, unused, unloved and empty. We had a few log burning stoves and one-bar electric fires in private rooms and dormitories, but whenever it was cold and everyone put on their heaters it overstretched the limited electricity supply and there was an inevitable power cut, just when heat was needed most. To make matters worse, not only was there no effective way of heating the building, but also many of the windows would not shut properly and all night a bitter wind howled through the gaps in the iron frames.

I was very pleased I had moved into one of the relatively comfortable visitor rooms for the month of the retreat.

Dorje, the Priory cat, was also delighted I was here, and in the freezing early hours of the morning she would rattle my door handle until I let her in. Without wasting any time she jumped into my bed and snuggled up closely for the rest of the night. From time to time she purred loudly and flexed and clenched her dainty little paws against my body – a way of expressing her affection I had mixed feelings about, especially as I had to get up before six while Dorje could sleep on peacefully as long as she liked.

Not being, by nature, a morning person, I found the

first session hard. And I usually returned to my room to wrap myself up warmly with a flask of coffee. All too soon it was time to leave the warm room and rush back up the stairs for more meditation. After a vegetarian lunch, I went on a quiet walk alone through the woods and down to the bay. I walked through wind, rain, snow and finally towards the end of January, a carpet of snowdrops.

Each evening, I took my stiff body, feeling more like cold streaky bacon than human flesh, to warm up in the shower before the final session of the day. I found the best way to do retreat was to do almost exactly the same in the breaks each day.

Making decisions about trivial matters took up valuable time and energy, and a pattern of behaviour naturally evolved. The last session was usually the best as I was warm and relaxed, but not so relaxed that I fell asleep.

Towards the end of the month it got harder, and at these times the silent support of the group was invaluable. No one missed a session, even though in those days the sessions were two hours long, and through their constancy and perseverance each retreater supported the whole group.

Speaking for myself I can say sitting in meditation is one of the most demanding and meaningful activities I have ever undertaken. Although it is true that ten or twenty minutes of meditation after a busy day can be pleasant and relaxing, this cannot be compared to true meditation done over a long period of time, which has the power to transform our self-centred mental habits into positive and peaceful states of mind. However it takes a lot of time and energy to change deeply entrenched habits.

How much my mind changed during that first retreat, I cannot say.

I did observe the days lengthening and the woods growing carpets of snowdrops, the birds starting to get excited about the oncoming spring and waking up earlier each day. It was very interesting to become aware of the subtle changes in the season even in one month, from the long dark days to the light and brighter days. What a perfect way to spend January. Even bears and hedgehogs do their little retreats each winter.

This retreat was a Tantric retreat. These days there is so much misunderstanding about Tantra. Many people seem to think Tantra is a method to improve their sex life and they can learn it on a weekend workshop (for which they have to have an AIDS test before joining!)

But this is not Buddhist Tantra. The purpose of Buddhist Tantra is exactly the same as the rest of Buddhism – to attain enlightenment for the benefit of all living beings. The methodology is different though and is extremely powerful, relying on complex visualisations and control over our inner energies.

Tantra is often called 'secret,' which makes some people suspicious and occasionally I am asked what the secret is. When they persist I say I would love to share the secret but I can't. Not because I am not allowed – all the Tantric practices I have been taught are explained in detail in Geshe Kelsang's books. However I cannot explain it because the real meaning of Tantra can only be experienced by a faithful practitioner after much effort and application.

Suppose I am standing at the bottom of my garden holding a book, and call to you, 'Can you see the book I am holding? Come closer and you will see the pictures better. Now come a bit closer and you will be able to make out the titles. Finally come closer still until you can read all the words and then you will understand what the story is about.'

Tantra is a bit like this. It is not difficult these days to read a bit about Tantra attend a workshop or receive a Tantric empowerment, but this is like seeing the pictures in my book from afar.

In order to fully understand the meaning of Tantra we need to get closer, and this is what the retreat was about. Coming closer involves becoming familiar with the practices, the prayers, the visualisations, and repeating the mantras many, many times with strong faith. This takes a lot of time, effort and above all patience. Although Tantra can be called the quick path, it is not for the impatient. In fact it is only quick for those who have had the patience to master its methods through long practice, and who have both an impeccable motivation and unshakeable faith in their Spiritual Guide.

I know people who, after a few months, or a year, or even ten or twenty years, become discouraged and give up their Tantric practice, saying that it does not work. This makes me very sad. Tantra has worked for thousands of years and still works now, but only when we let it into our hearts.

At times I feel that my own Tantric practice will not bring results in this life. But I can say from my own experience the more wholeheartedly I practice the happier I am, and the less energy I put into my practice of Tantra the less I enjoy it. My teacher says that a Buddhist practitioner should be like a child at play, thoroughly absorbed and enjoying their games. When children are playing they are not constantly worrying about achieving results. They do not ask their mother, 'Is it time to stop playing now?'

The final destination of Tantra is eternal peace and joy, and the path itself is peaceful and joyful. When I finally reach this destination I can help bring everyone to the same place.

Although few people admit it, deep down most know they are suffering. Why else would they put so much effort into seeking happiness? Do I need the latest phone to be happy?

Obviously not; I am just trying to fill the emptiness that gnaws away inside my mind. But a phone cannot fill the void as a phone is a physical object and so can never fill my non-physical mind. Lacking wisdom, people seek fulfilment in distractions such as alcohol, drugs and television, or dream of holidays to take away the boredom and pain of an unfulfilled life. In spite of his wealth Mick Jagger could: '... get no satisfaction ...'

Yet the road to satisfaction is open to everyone, even to the materially destitute. Seven years after our first Tantric retreat with Geshe-la at the institute he left for Scotland and began a three year retreat. I would have liked to join him but for personal reasons could not and so I stayed at the Institute.

After he left I led the customary winter retreat, but a year later my throat still hurt from so much Tibetan chanting and I decided for a change to look for a suitable cottage to do my own private retreat throughout the winter and then return to Manjushri at Easter. This seemed an exciting plan, and I began by looking for a cottage to rent in Eskdale, my favourite valley in the Lake District. Eventually I found a wonderful little cottage on Penny Hill Farm, formerly the property of Beatrix Potter but now owned by the National Trust.

My winter retreat began and I spent the next seven months alone in this delightful little valley, the only other occupants being the farmer and his family next door. My milk supply wandered about in the small field in front of the cottage.

Flopsy the Friesian provided my drink and entertainment, and when she had her calf, her mother, Daisy, who was a beautiful soft brown Jersey, fostered it so Flopsy could continue to supply milk to the farm.

The cock, hens and ducks clucked and quacked about the farmyard. This was the farm of every child's favourite book. There were dogs of every shape and size. Laddy was a large and independent foxhound who had seen better days. Nip the opportunist took every chance to nip into my cottage when my back was turned and he even had the cheek to get up on the chair and sleep in comfort while I went on my daily walk. This must have been quite a change for him as usually he shared the hay in the barn with hens and whatever other animals happened to be there at the time. Sneaky dog!

All the dogs were working dogs except Laddy who had retired. It was wonderful to see how they shared their food, which was prepared in the kitchen by Margaret, the farmer's wife, and served on the farmhouse doorstep in a big dish. The dogs crowded round taking it in turns to put their heads in the dish and then moved back to let other dogs join in, so that all of them, from the senior dogs to the puppies, got what they needed.

In this way the puppies learned table manners at an early age. After that the collies had to return to their kennels and be locked in to stop them wandering off and getting lost. Speck was a sheep dog who refused to work with sheep, while the puppy loved to practice his skill at every opportunity. It was strange to see how the sheep obeyed the tiny dog no bigger than a rabbit, as he squeezed under the field gate to practice his shepherding by rounding up the pregnant ewes. There was also the naughty little white goat who fostered the orphan lambs.

Throughout the winter I meditated and wrote my notes for hours at a time in the little cottage, going on hill walks whenever the weather permitted.

I had chosen this magic valley as I had no transport

and the Eskdale railway station was only a mile from the farm. Once a day Ratty, the miniature train, rattled down the hillside for seven miles to Ravenglass on the coast, returning in the evening. Sometimes I got up at five in the morning and walked by torchlight to the little station to catch the train at six and return in the evening. My walk took me past the bull-field. As I walked along the deserted farm track and over Doctor Bridge; so called because in the past the doctor had lived on this side of the river Esk and needed to get to his patients on the other side when they were ill. Now that the bridge had been built he could cross even when the river was in flood.

Thanks to that doctor, I walked over the bridge and turned left along the winding road that descended from the old Roman Fort of Hard Knot in a series of hairpin bends. I tried hard not to think of the escaped bulls and cows that would surely be waiting to greet me round each dark corner. Fortunately all I ever met was the occasional wandering sheep, but in the dark they sounded very much like bulls.

At last safely on the platform, Ratty the little train, which had been parked by the driver's railway cottage over night, pulled into the station.

I boarded the miniature train, bought a return ticket from the driver, and found a dusty seat amongst the wheelbarrows and shovels. When Ratty reached Ravenglass, seven miles down the line, the driver went to the depot where he would spend the rest of the day maintaining the delightful little trains. Rattled and frozen by the cold drafty journey to Ravenglass, I crossed to the main line station and caught the train to Ulverston.

At four o'clock the driver would return home, parking Ratty outside his cottage door for another night.

These days, I believe the miniature train runs commercially throughout the year, doing Santa trips in the winter, which are very popular with small children and grannies alike. Recently I met one of these grannies lamenting that her grandchildren had become too big for this treat. She was now hoping to take the neighbour's children for their treat, but unfortunately all the tickets had been sold.

My own reason for being here in Eskdale was not so popular. Few people are attracted to such a solitary and outwardly uneventful life. Many spend their entire life wandering from distraction to distraction but never finding fulfilment in the brief pleasures they come across. Knowing this, I must not fritter away my own life on a succession of meaningless activities, but remember at all times I am living in the shadow of the lord of death. This is not morbid, nor is it sad. It is liberating!

A small part of this journey began on my first day at school and throughout my school days I felt trapped in a system where I felt like an alien, and where the need to ingest tiresome and trivial facts seemed to suffocate me almost verging on physical pain. Writing pages of useless information hurt; not my fingers, but my mind. It felt like this torture would never end. But it was not for me, a mere child, to question why I needed to suffer like this.

At the end of the winter I returned to Manjushri, to find that everyone was excited about a new course which was beginning this spring, a Teacher Training course designed for westerners who wanted to teach Buddhism. I am not by nature a scholar, and when Joan, a friend asked me if I was going to join this new study class, without hesitation I said no, I was not; I was planning to do a long retreat.

I went to the office to explain the reason why I would not join, but the Director of Education saw no contradiction. I found Jim, the teacher, and asked him if we could discuss the new programme which was to begin the next day. He explained that an interview would not be necessary as I had already done many years of study so I should just turn up the next morning. I wanted to stamp my foot and scream, 'No!'

Why did everyone assume I would be joining them?

Had I not studied enough in this life? I definitely did not want to study, I wanted to meditate. The idea of formal study and regular exams sounded too much like school and I had thought my examination days were over.

The following day I sat down with the rest of the students to begin the course. The commitment was to complete all of it without a break once it was begun. The trouble was no one knew how long it would take. Not all the textbooks had been written yet. It turned out that I spent the next fifteen years of my life studying my way through twelve books. As I had never decided to do this course in the first place, I reasoned it was not possible for me to change my mind. The years rolled on and I struggled on with my ever diminishing eyesight. But in retrospect I can't think of a more meaningful way to have spent the time and I have no doubt that without this formal commitment I would not have even opened some of these books.

It can't be denied that in Buddhism there is an awful lot of philosophy, but I reasoned perhaps I need all this theory, after all I had not been brought up in a Buddhist country and if I wanted to do a long retreat then I first needed a clear idea of how to meditate.

Buddhism is called a vehicle because it takes us to our spiritual destination. But this internal vehicle is much more sophisticated than little Ratty the miniature train.

And the destination it can take me to is infinitely further than any I can reach by train. So why am I so reluctant to make the effort to take a closer look at this path to my final destination? After all, being a student is a process not a product. The final result is to attain enlightenment; and when I reach it there will be no need to study any more. I can leave behind all the books, philosophy and debate.

Sometimes when I contemplate these points I am reminded of a game of snakes and ladders, the difference being this is not a game of chance and all the dangerous snakes are in my mind. That's why I need to study and meditate so deeply – to get rid of all those crazy snakes.

The following autumn another cottage owner telephoned me and asked if I would like to stay in his cottage. How could I turn down such an irresistible offer? So I spent the next four months in the tiny village of Boot. But as I now had a commitment to do the Teacher Training Programme, when term began I travelled to Manjushri for the classes and returned on the Ratty each weekend. But I found the travelling difficult in the cold winter months.

When the following year a letter landed on my doorstep inviting me back to the magic valley I could not resist the temptation, and went to do a further few weeks retreat in a cottage on Hollins Farm in Eskdale. This time however, I intended to return to Manjushri in February to begin the new term.

When I returned to Manjushri Institute I was offered a caravan to live in at the bottom of the kitchen garden. Throughout this time Venerable Geshe Kelsang was still engaged in his own three year retreat in Tharpaland, his retreat centre in the hills near Dumfries in southern Scotland. Although he had asked me to join him and I would have loved nothing more than to spend time with him and the nine or ten fortunate disciples who were doing retreat with him, I felt it would not be fair to leave Paula in England until she was older, even if she was cared for materially by others. I was after all her mother.

Finally Geshe-la had returned from Scotland and Paula was older. I was now ready for my big retreat. Three years in Scotland.

It had been a long, hot and difficult summer, packed with exciting things to do. I had attended the summer course and learnt how to make a sand mandala in the traditional Tibetan way.

But after a few months living in the caravan in the peaceful kitchen garden, amongst the cabbages and sprouts, my little home was due to be removed from the Manjushri kitchen garden and sold as there was no planning permission for it to remain. Now my little home was about to be lifted over the garden wall by a large crane, and I felt that the time had definitely come to start my three year retreat.

I remained at Manjushri for the autumn course: The Bodhisattva Vow, which I particularly wanted to attend.

With great encouragement from Geshe Kelsang, as soon as the course ended I packed my belongings into a car and sped off to Tharpaland. My retreat began in earnest in November nineteen eighty-nine. In addition to the study programme, which I continued throughout the retreat, I planned to do eight hours of meditation each day.

My aim on this retreat was to complete the nine traditional preliminary practices described in Geshe-la's book, *Guide to Dakini Land*. This was very demanding and to the best of my knowledge had not yet been completed in the west. So it was a mixture of following an ancient tradition and spiritual pioneering.

The decision to do this retreat had been mine alone, and I wished to follow the classic example of a retreat as done in India or Tibet.

Each day began at six with one hundred prostrations. My body hated these but I knew if I waited until after breakfast it would hate them more as my breakfast was likely to rattle about and make itself felt in an uncomfortable manner. Prostrations are an important practice of purification and I was determined to complete the traditional one hundred thousand, regardless of the discomfort.

After this I meditated for a couple of hours, followed by breakfast and a short walk to blow away the cobwebs. I was then ready for the rest of the days study and meditation.

Having worked out the structure of each day, all I had to do was to repeat the same pattern for the next three years. What could be easier? What could be harder!

Some of the retreat was designed to purify negative karma, some to accumulate merit, and some to receive the blessings of the Buddhas. There is a traditional analogy to explain these three functions. If a farmer wants to harvest a good crop, he must first prepare the field by getting rid of the rocks and weeds, which corresponds to the practice of purification. Then he must fertilise it, which corresponds to the practice of accumulating merit. Finally he must ensure that the field is well irrigated, which corresponds to receiving the blessings of the Buddhas. In a field which has been cleaned, manured and watered, he can then plant his seeds. This corresponds to the actual practice of meditation.

In the west so many people are interested in Buddhist meditation, but few understand the importance of first preparing their mind through the preliminary practices. All the great Lamas of Tibet insist on the importance of the preliminaries. Ignoring their advice if I just try to meditate, my efforts will not bear fruit.

Each of the nine preliminary practices should be repeated one hundred thousand times. Nine hundred thousand was an inconceivably large number, but if I did one hundred prostrations each morning it would feel less daunting. As for the remaining eight, I could complete them one at a time. I began with one hundred thousand refuge prayers.

Shortly after I began my retreat, Paula moved to Hastings so she could be close to her Grandma and David's family and not be a nuisance while I was in retreat. However during this time she met her husband and had her first child, Jessica.

I could not miss these important events in her life; after all I was not only a retreater, I was also a mother and three years is too long to be apart from a daughter. So I made the long journey to the South Coast for her wedding. Later on I visited my first grandchild.

I had been concerned for the welfare of my ageing parents but throughout the retreat they remained in good health.

In general it is not good to interrupt a retreat, but family commitments are also important. Perhaps in a different culture like Tibet where people understand the importance of retreat it was possible to be stricter, but had I refused to go to Paula's wedding or visit my first grandchild, my family would not have understood and I felt it was important to respect their values and not offend them, or let Paula down.

Perhaps in a previous incarnation I may have been a retreater in India or Tibet, and I am sure in such a strict retreat my teacher would not have approved of this distraction from my routine, but in this life I am not a man walled up in a cave and I am glad not to be so extreme.

Instead I am trying to follow the middle way between the extremes of materialism and spirituality.

As it was, I did not find these 'interruptions' much of a problem and as soon as I got back to Tharpaland I went straight back into retreat; more energised than distracted.

On completing the recitation of one hundred thousand refuge prayers, my mind was calm and peaceful. I was even enjoying my study and preparing for the next exam was not difficult.

Soon after, I began the preparation for the preliminary of mandala offerings. I knew this practice would be a long one as it consists of offering heaps of rice mentally transformed into the whole universe which is then offered to the Buddhas visualised in the space in front of me.

This is the traditional method to generate merit and I certainly felt I could do with some more merit. As I became familiar with this routine I found my mind was drawn towards a close friend and this was becoming a big distraction.

As this thought disturbed my meditation I resolved to destroy this phantom; the enemy in my mind and wrote a letter wishing he find happiness somewhere else.

Perhaps he did or perhaps he did not; I genuinely

wanted him to be happy. But what mattered more was, that once the letter was posted the distracting thoughts melted away. Now with a greater sense of freedom I returned to my meditation and was able to concentrate without distraction after that.

The days, weeks and months rolled by and the counting continued. Seven months later I counted the final mandala, elated by this wonderful practice of giving.

Materially of course I had given nothing to anyone.

But all of life is just a series of exchanges between people, some physical, some verbal and some mental. Making mandala offerings was no different; it was an exchange between me and all the Buddhas, and my body, speech and mind were involved in making offerings to them. Even though it was done in the imagination, making mandala offerings is a powerful method to train in the mental attitude of giving.

Because we mentally give the whole universe to the Buddhas, holding nothing back, our hearts are open and freed from attachment. Through this wonderful practice I would receive greater merit than if I gave material gifts to hundreds of people; after all material gifts can only create happiness for a very short time.

But if I complete the first of the six perfections, the perfection of giving, I shall be capable of giving others anything they ask for without a sense of loss, and will quickly progress to full enlightenment.

By now I had forgotten what day of the week it was. Nights, days and even seasons blended together; I did not want to leave this familiar routine behind. I had enjoyed making these offerings. But now I needed to let go and move on to the next part of my retreat.

As my back hurt I rested it while doing a short hundred thousand Samayavajra mantra counting retreat to purify any mistakes I had made so far with regard to my Spiritual Guide, before starting the Purification of Vajrasattva.

Winter approached; my health was affected by the cold damp weather. The nights were long and cold, the days short and dark; but perhaps this afforded fewer distractions than the long, warm days when the sun hardly slept before dawn lit up the summer sky again. So I struggled on in the hope that my spiritual progress would lighten my days. But this mantra was difficult to recite and my memory for it dark and heavy. The long nights were filled with pain that left me sleepless. However, as this was a practice of purification I reasoned that like taking unpleasant medicine for a physical illness, perseverance was the cure and I would definitely improve. Meanwhile I studied Clear Light of Bliss in preparation for the next exam.

It was hard at first, very hard as I was constantly cold and tired, but after a couple of months the long mantra became easier to recite.

As the cold dark winter made way for the bright, green spring and little lambs filled up the nearby fields again, the counting continued until the day the clocks changed to British Summer Time and at last I counted the final mantras. This was definitely cause for rejoicing after the winter months.

It seemed that the lamas regarded one hundred thousand as a special number. Until I had completed all of these it was not for me to judge. Even then, I would possibly not notice the results in this life. Having said this, the more familiar I became with each practice the more interesting and enjoyable it became. Each one produced a very different feeling from the others.

I had no doubt how privileged I was to be given the opportunity to do this retreat. Perhaps I can compare it to a journey which was demanding, but also fun. Like a great adventure, exploring the unknown recesses of my mind.

At this time a team of noisy builders arrived at Tharpaland to explore the damp and dry rot in the darkest and deepest corners of the building before damp-proofing it. However filling the cavities in the walls of the building was somewhat noisier than filling the cavities of my mind with positive thoughts.

So I moved to Auchencheyne, a farm in Moniaive, and continued my retreat.

At this point I concluded a retreat was not a place but a state of mind, and I soon began offering water to the Buddhas on this peaceful and beautiful farm. It is said that whenever someone imagines a Buddha with faith, immediately they are there. They are not restricted by time or distance.

Water. Why water? Even the poorest people can afford pure water, but I felt there was more to water offerings than mere liquid.

Water is one of the four elements. When I made mandala offerings, I offered rice, which arose from the earth; Vajradaka was a burning offering where black sesame seeds were burned as an offering to the fire deity Vajradaka to purify faults and downfalls; and mantras were sacred sounds and composed of air. All four elements are needed to be kept in perfect balance and harmony as they are essential for the health of my body and mind. They are equally important for the health of our planet. A planet in which the elements are in balance cannot promote disease and there will be peace and harmony among the population; whereas a planet filled with greed and anger will upset the balance of the four elements, causing disasters such as earthquakes, floods, fires and storms.

Yes, it was good to give pure water and I developed a deep respect for it. On this farm the water was collected in a small reservoir to supply the farm and offering such purity felt good.

I must have done something right to be born in a place where clean water was freely available, while millions of people die due to the lack of clean water.

At the moment I have no power to help them or save their lives; my main job is to overcome the anger and ignorance in my own mind. Perhaps as a result of making these offerings and developing the wish that all who need water can find pure drinking water, other people will be inspired to help those who are desperate and dying in drought ravaged countries with failed crops and empty reservoirs. I can only pray someone with the ability to do so will give them water. For my part, I can't do that but I can try to attain enlightenment to become a Buddha, and then help others by showing them the path of compassion.

The last and most demanding and exciting of the nine preliminary practices was making one hundred thousand Buddha images. This took eighteen months. Even before moving into Manjushri I had wanted to set up a pottery to make Buddha images. Now, after fifteen years waiting, I still had no kiln but would be able to make them in plaster.

I had moulds made from little brass statues of Buddha Shakyamuni, Dorje Shugden and Vajrayogini, but making the plaster statues from these moulds was quite fiddly and they were time consuming to paint. What I needed was a plaque with several Buddha images on it as the work would then speed up. Manjushri Institute's resident sculptor explained what I needed to do and I set about making a plaque of the thirty-five Confession Buddhas, similar to the painting found on the front cover of the first edition of Geshe-la's book The Bodhisattva Vow.

I am a painter but had never turned my hand to sculpting, so the plaque took me two months to complete; in the end I was satisfied I had done my best, and had six silicone moulds made.

I now had all the moulds I needed, and several sacks of high quality plaster and gold paint.

In total, I probably used about thirty sacks of plaster. In Tibet they would have had to dig their own clay, and gather the wood to fire it. But luckily I could buy everything over the phone with a credit card.

Perhaps I had had the choice to make fewer statues, but this never occurred to me, and I had said I would make all of them. Now, it had to be one hundred thousand or die.

I had spent years dreaming about making one hundred thousand. My dream was now about to come true. This was an opportunity to create some merit and it was going to be a great adventure. It would not be like the little yellow merit badges I had sported with pride in La Sagesse school when I was a junior student, but a great collection which I now realised I desperately needed.

People with a lot of merit can easily fulfil their wishes, both spiritual and mundane. But life up until now had been a constant struggle to make ends meet, and despite many years of practising meditation I could not boast any great realisations. These were perfect indications I lacked merit.

At first the work was painfully slow and I felt I would surely die before it was finished. The one word which kept bubbling up in my mind was impossible.

In order to avoid that defeatist word, I played tricks with my mind; instead of overwhelming myself with the thought of having to make so many, I gave myself a commitment to make just five thousand. When I had finished these and reached that goal I congratulated myself and rejoiced, then I continued up to ten thousand. When I'd completed these I told myself someone who could make ten thousand could make twenty thousand. Now a quarter of the total was in sight, and in no time at all I reached twenty five thousand. Someone who could count a quarter could count a half.

In this way, the donkey of my mind moved forward, sometimes reluctantly and sometimes joyfully.

I had some delightful little books to record my efforts. Once fifty thousand had been reached I reasoned that, like any other mountain climber, I now had only to descend down the other side and had already proved I could cover that distance. And of course, as I progressed the work became easier.

I had discovered that on retreat it is best to begin each new practice slowly and gently. When I familiarised myself with the practice it naturally became quicker. After reciting a mantra over each one and dipping it in gold paint they were ready to join the Buddha family in my spare room.

Days, weeks and months rolled by. I became more efficient in my Buddha factory, but as the room filled up I fancied I could hear the rich and powerful sounds of joyful Tibetan chanting.

Every day was spent in the same way and rarely did I see anyone during that time, but how could I be lonely in the company of so many Buddhas?

Through a combination of mixing powder and water together a Buddha was born. And it was no less exciting than the birth of a child. Thousands each day were coming into our world and each one as exciting as the last.

This way of living for the benefit of all was more exciting than anything I had ever done. I would not deny that it was hard and even affected my health but I felt alive! At last I was doing something really worthwhile with my life. I have not felt the same way since then.

Although I still do a regular month-long, strict, retreat each January, during which time I feel I am doing what I really need to do with my life, throughout the remaining eleven months I often feel I am frittering my life away on meaningless pastimes.

There are three types of retreat. The first is according to time. For example, deciding to do retreat for a month or for three years. The second, which I was near to completing, is according to number; and in this counting retreat I had planned to count nine hundred thousand preliminary practices, regardless of how long it took. The days and months flew by. After about four and a half years, I had made nine hundred thousand offerings prostrations mantras and images and completed my long retreat. What a wonderful feeling! Now I knew this retreat, which had seemed almost impossible, could be done, even by a middle aged blind woman with low reserves of energy. Although in the end, the three year retreat took me four and a half years, as it was a counting retreat, I would have broken my retreat commitment if I had not counted every single preliminary I had promised to do.

As a result in the future I might have found it difficult to fulfil such promises. But by keeping my promise I had now prepared the ground for a further retreat.

The third type of retreat is according to realisation. The ultimate challenge! My previous retreats were called preliminaries because they were paving the way for this one.

When Shakyamuni Buddha went off into the forest and sat under the Bodhi tree he had vowed to remain until he attained this realisation. But am I ready for enlightenment right now?

One of the most difficult aspects of the path to

enlightenment these days is the development of perfect concentration, known as tranquil abiding. Our lives are so busy and filled with distractions, and our attention spans so short, that the inner stillness of meditative concentration is far harder to achieve nowadays than it used to be in the past. To achieve tranquil abiding one needs to pass through nine levels of concentration. My teacher advises me that we develop the first four levels in our daily meditation sessions during our ordinary life. When we have achieved the fourth level we can remain focused on our object of meditation for the entire meditation session of forty minutes or an hour, without forgetting the object even once. We are then ready to do a strict meditation retreat to achieve the remaining five stages and then tranquil abiding itself. This is said to take six months, but could take quite a lot longer in these degenerate times. Would I be able to develop the fourth level of concentration in my daily life and then gather all the conditions needed to complete a tranquil abiding retreat?

I was so grateful to have had the good fortune to complete the distant preliminaries and hopefully purify many of the obstacles awaiting me on this journey.

Preparing for a long retreat takes much time and energy, but coming out of retreat felt quite strange. Strange in that there was a feeling that I should still be doing my daily intensive practice. Strange, in that everyone was four years older. Life had gone on quite well without me. Perhaps I should have been happy about this; perhaps I should have felt hurt.

The world had moved forward during that time and I felt like an alien with no conversation of interest to anyone. But if I was an alien I was a stronger alien.

And after all, I had always been an alien, unable to join in with family games and out of touch with current events. Perhaps it is better to be an alien than to get seduced by day-to-day problems. A detached mind is a balanced mind, and love without attachment the goal of the Bodhisattva. So I should be content not to be the life and soul of the party but just an observer sitting on the side. Rather like a mother happy to watch her children playing in a park, knowing that they are oblivious of her needs, but they will come when they feel hungry and realise it is time for tea.

Now I needed to turn my attention to my wonderful Buddha family. It was time for them to move on.

The spare room was filled to capacity and they could not remain indefinitely. So on the advice of my teacher, I gave them as a gift to Manjushri Centre, carefully boxed and wrapped to protect their shiny gold paint. A monk drove them to the Centre and soon a small army of monks and nuns were found to unload the van and carry them into the chapel. At this time there was an international teacher training course in Manjushri Centre, and the teachers took many of the little statues home with them. As my family left to travel all over the world, I tried to develop a mind of detachment as I watched the boxes disappearing through the large chapel doors. Now that my Buddha family had dispersed, I could think of them as a global family.

A few years later a wonderful use was found for some of the remaining Buddha plaques. A temple big enough for two thousand people was built in the old walled garden of Manjushri Centre – where my caravan had previously stood– and several large Buddha statues were being made for the shrine, the largest of which being eight feet high. According to Buddhist tradition, Buddha statues are always filled with precious objects. So along with dried flowers and printed mantras, my Buddha images were placed inside the statues.

I was told that there would be one thousand in the

largest Buddha statue in the centre of the temple.

Now every time someone bows down to the statue, they are in fact prostrating to one thousand and one Buddhas, although only one is visible. Remembering this makes me very happy, even though these days I can't even see the large Buddha.

I remained in Scotland for several more years continuing to study the Teacher Training Programme. Few people can commit themselves to fifteen years of continual study, and I frequently became tired of the demanding programme. Over the years my eyesight had been getting steadily worse and I often had to find new ways of accessing printed matter. At first I made enlarged photocopies of the text as I could no longer read normal size print. Gradually my double vision got so bad that I had to cover up one eye to read or write.

Eventually I could no longer read at all but luckily by this time talking computers had been invented. So, although it was a challenge and study got harder and harder, I still kept up with the rest of the students.

Although most of the time I studied on my own, my presence in Manjushri Centre was required fairly regularly and travelling from Dumfries was getting more difficult. I loved living in Scotland, but I needed to be closer to Manjushri in Cumbria.

Just then a friend told me about a 'luxury apartment' to let nearby and although I didn't feel I needed much luxury I telephoned to make enquiries. It was right on the shore of Morecambe Bay and only a short walk to Manjushri. It was so peaceful, I could not ask for more.

But I did get more; I got my beautiful guide dog, Sage, together we explored the woods and the bay, but more than that she brought so much happiness into my life and the lives of others as she was such a happy dog and loved everyone that she met.

That winter I joined the group retreat in January. It was nice to have others to share the retreat again after so much solitude. The month passed quickly, the days lengthened and snowdrops carpeted the woods again.

When the opportunity to move to a detached lodge came up, I took it hoping my family would enjoy the lovely house and garden. They did come occasionally. But during the summer festival of two thousand and six, I made a sudden decision to move out of the lodge. I would of course not find another house with a stream running through the garden, and Sage my delightful guide dog and I would miss paddling in it or crossing over the little bridge and into the bluebell woods. But my time would be better spent living quietly, meditating and studying at my own pace, rather than paddling in the stream with Sage.

Three weeks later I found Glebe Cottage on a private estate in the upper Tyne Valley. Sage and I are enjoying life in the hills. I am told that locally 'glebe' means small grassy mound. Perhaps this is the one that I used to daydream of during my early school days when I dreamed of becoming a philosopher! And although I am still looking for the meaning of life, now I have a map I trust.

Chapter 12

'BYE-BYE'

In spite of the passage of time I have not lost touch with Mary, my best friend, from the junior school in La Sagesse [Daughters of Wisdom] when we were learning to be young ladies. But now when she visits I have to be mindful of what I say as I am so used to Buddhist terminology and it would sound strange to anyone unfamiliar with it. However although the words may be different, and there are many different ways of expressing it; there is only one type of wisdom.

We both know the wisdom of our childhood is losing its power in favour of advances in technology and if the people of this world do not develop wisdom now, in the future there will be no one to teach it to others.

The two thousand and nine Summer Festival was the biggest, the most international, and the saddest: the one I had been dreading for some time. After thirty years of tireless teaching my Guru was retiring.

Although I had attended all the festivals at Manjushri, each year I saw less and less. In fact, my eyesight was by now so bad that I had not seen my teacher or the powerful statues and paintings that adorned the temple for many years. But fortunately I have a good visual memory and imagination, and many years of gazing devotedly at Buddha images while I could still see, have left them etched deep in my heart.

Thirty years of teachings, personal advice, empowerments and blessings, given freely and with such consummate skill and love; seeds of Buddhahood planted in my mind by this master gardener of the soul.

It was now up to me to tend these little plants, their tender shoots of wisdom struggling up through the mud of my mind, drawn by the light filtering through the murky water, until finally they will emerge into the bright wisdom light of day, and the buds open into beautiful lotus blossoms.

Seeds of Buddhahood like golden jewels,
Hidden in the depths of my dark mind,
Now to be watered with my own compassion and wisdom.
As the lotus in my heart gradually opens,
Revealing soft white velvet petals,
Floating gently on the surface of my crystal clear mind,
And reaching upwards to the clear blue sky.
I will then be able to invite a swarm of thirsty bees to feast
On the wisdom nectar that drips from the stamens in the centre of the Lotus,
The priceless golden nectar of my own root Guru's speech.
I must live in solitude on windswept heights
And under starlit skies,
Seeking to perfect my mind,
Until finally the physical form of the teacher,
but not the teachings are left behind.

And so I must move on and prepare for further retreat. After all, my previous retreat of four and a half years was called a 'preliminary retreat.' Since then I have been finding out what it was a preliminary to. I must prepare well but not wait too long, as I cannot know how much longer my body or mind will be strong enough for the rigors of retreat. While I still have the opportunity I must take the real meaning of this human life by preparing for my future lives, putting my thirty years of Buddhism into practice for the benefit of others.

For the first thirty years of my life my wisdom eyes were blind. I had no idea what direction to take, or what advice to listen to.

But I had the good fortune to be baptised into the Catholic Church and taught how to live a moral life. As a Catholic I had taken part in some wonderful uplifting services with many loving friends and kind people who had helped to shape my life. I was fortunate enough to be able to paint and draw well, which gave me some insight and depth into the lives of others. I was able to care for my demented grandmother for a while, the lady who taught me true humility but surely there had to be more.

Then I met my Buddhist teachers, above all my root Guru Geshe Kelsang Gyatso, who lived in Cumbria and gave teachings throughout the year. For the next thirty years I listened to his teachings but am also willing to accept little pearls of wisdom from any quarter, Buddhist or non-Buddhist. I am still trying to gain wisdom from life's little dramas wherever they may be, and live in harmony with people whatever their beliefs.

It is sometimes difficult to fit together the pieces of the jigsaw of life, but when I could, there was always a great sense of achievement, a sense of personal purpose I had never experienced in the past.

Now my wisdom eyes are beginning to open to the laws of cause and effect, or karma, and to the importance of future lives.

I am also developing an unshakeable respect for others. Out of ignorance I may still hurt or offend them, but there is no place for the negative mind of guilt in Buddhism, an emotion that serves only to disempower me.

I cannot alter past mistakes, but I can take them as my teachers, giving me council on how to act in the future. While recognising the faults I have I must not dwell on them unnecessarily, but put great effort into developing positive minds. Then even my guilty secrets can become my teachers.

In July of two thousand and nine, Manjushri Centre was bracing itself for the biggest international festival that they had ever organised. The last opportunity to listen to our Tibetan teacher. But after two weeks of teachings and meditation, given to an international crowd of thousands, there was no great speech, no grand ceremony of farewell. Just two simple words: 'Bye bye.'

As the eyes of thousands of students misted over, I tried to grasp the real meaning of these two short words. Geshe-la promised to remain with us mentally, always, but physically he was not going to return to Manjushri Centre here in England and if I wished to sit at his feet and listen to his instruction I would have to travel abroad. This would not be possible without the help of others and the sense of loss is difficult to bear. I did not have the opportunity to say bye-bye to his earthly form. But so often he has explained to us that according to the Buddhist teaching, an earthly form is just like a house, somewhere to live for a limited time until it becomes too old for habitation. Then we need to move on to the next house. But the question is what will we take with us?

When I vacate the house of my body, it is my heartfelt hope I will take with me the faith, hope and charity I had been taught in La Sagesse School when I was a small child and the wisdom and compassion taught by my Buddhist teachers in later years; as well as all the personal advice Geshe la and others have bestowed on me over the years through their teaching and example. But to be able to do this I need to make these instructions my own, to plant them deep inside my own heart so that they transform me, until I become wisdom; become compassion. If I can do this then my human life will have been truly meaningful.

So Lyndhurst, our happy family home, where as a small child I had felt safe from unknown things; Teddy and all my other friends; all the people and places and events I have loved and lost since then are like a river of molten iron softened in the heat of the furnace of life, but now frozen in my memory. Although having no substance, they are the only tools with which I can shape my future. And if I allow them, they have the power to generate delusions and freeze my progress towards my future lives.

When I learn to light the fire of eternal love in my heart
My delusions dazzled by the bright flames
Will cry for mercy.

But I will show them no mercy:
There will be no mercy for my dark minds,
As they wave their angry banners aloft,
Seeking to pour icy black water to extinguish
compassion and love.
Masquerading as friends, they destroy all joy
And crush compassion with wily words and false
promises.
But I shall light a furnace in my mind,
Filling it with love to melt these icy enemies.
Their frosty fingers will not harm me then.
I will melt this very body until all that remains is a
pool of love.
Those hungry for happiness can then feast on the
nectar that poured down from my Guru's heart,
And overflowed, filling Heaven and earth.
This cold body transformed into a glorious temple,
Filling and fulfilling the dreams of all who
encounter it.
Heaven beyond conception, full of flowers and
jewels of every kind,
Free to everyone with pure love's mind.
Until my heart explodes into a million fragments
and a million million more,
To fulfil the needs of needy people
And protect them forever more.
Heavenly perfumes will fill the air
When goddesses sing sweetly and offer praises
And the timeless sound of flutes fill ten directions.
I will dance in the glorious light of death,
The light that outshines all worldly pleasure and
pain.

At the moment I am entrenched in petty problems,
day to day things. I have a long way to go before I can
abide in such joyful states, before I can truly help

limitless beings with my own wisdom. Wisdom born of the wise words of my teachers, the harvest of the seeds they have sown in the field of my mind. If I do not fertilise these seeds with my own wisdom and water them with my own compassion, then there will be no harvest of wisdom to take with me to my next life, no compassionate and loving mind to cherish future beings. So regardless of the lives and loves of others, I must love them all and seek the wisdom that lies in every man's heart.

If I fail, the icy claws of the Lord of Death will freeze the fiery furnace of my heart, and I shall go to my next life empty handed, confused and filled with fear. But if I succeed, I will walk tall and fearless, melting everything dark along my path with wisdom's golden glow, a powerful protector of all who I meet. The choice is mine. I want to make my Guru proud, proud to have me as his student. And I ask for his blessing to fulfil my dream.

Lightning Source UK Ltd
Milton Keynes UK
UKOW06f1858201115

263165UK00011B/74/P